"I recommend this book for those experienced clinical practitioners who have made it beyond the panicked search for techniques in this field—as a reminder of the real risks involved in change. For those still engaged in that search, it is required reading."

—David J. Clark, PHD., S.C.A.C.
Co-director, GIFT Training Institute

"One gets the sense from Sober Spring of the range of feelings and frustrations that not only the alcoholic but also the family and loved ones go through in dealing with this deadly disease. It clearly points out that there is no 'bad guy' and paints a picture of the warm personalities and real people that are involved."

—Joseph E. Troiani, M.A., C.A.C.
Administrator, CAREUNIT of DuPage

"Sober Spring belongs in the hands of all who work with hurting people, who have situations in the home which require confrontation, and anyone who has a desire to understand and help in the healing process of those who come into their lives."

—Regis Walling
Upper Peninsula Catholic

SOBER SPRING

One Family's Battle With Addiction

Robert Bollendorf

AUGSBURG   *Minneapolis*
ACTA   *Chicago*

SOBER SPRING
One Family's Battle with Addiction

Published by Augsburg, 426 South Fifth St., Box 1209, Minneapolis, MN 55440 and ACTA Publications, 4848 N. Clark St., Chicago, IL 60640.

Cover design: Lecy Design
Text design and typography: LINK Book Development and Production

---

Library of Congress Cataloging-in-Publication Data

Bollendorf, Robert F.
    Sober spring : one family's battle with addiction / Robert
Bollendorf.
            p.   cm.
    Reprint. Originally published: Chicago, Ill. : Buckley
Publications, c1988.
        Augsburg ISBN 0-8066-2539-2
        ACTA ISBN 0-915388-32-4
        1. Alcoholics—Wisconsin—Family relationships—Case studies.
    2. Alcoholics—Rehabilitation—Wisconsin—Case studies.   3. Co-
    dependence (Psychology)—Wisconsin—Case studies.   I. Title.
    HV5132.B65   1991
    362.29'23—dc20   91-17474
                                                            CIP

The paper used in this publication meets the minimum requirements of American National Standard for Information Sciences–Permanence of Paper for Printed Library Materials, ANSI Z329, 48-1984.   ∞™

Manufactured in the U.S.A.   AF 9-2539

95   94   93   92   91   1   2   3   4   5   6   7   8   9   10

Dedication

It seems at crucial beginnings of my life, there was a person named Fred there to help me along and show me the ropes. When I started my life there was my father. When I started my career there was Fred Holbeck, who became my mentor. Finally when I became interested in the disease of alcoholism and how it affects the family there was Fred Klein. This book is dedicated to them and their families.

Acknowledgments

I~T scares me that I may forget to mention one or more of the people who played a significant part in the writing of this book. To you I must apologize. If it's any consolation, I'll probably wake up some night and remember you and not get back to sleep because of the guilt I feel. It is also difficult to determine who contributed the most, so I've decided to name people in the order—to the best of my recollection—in which they entered my story, rather than by their relative importance.

To start with, I'd like to note some of the people who were involved in the field of intervention and/or working with chemically dependent families before me. My thanks to Elmer Johnson for developing an "intervention" in the first place. Thanks to Claudia Black and Sharon Wegscheider for their early work with dependent families.

On a more personal note, I guess I'd first have to start with my sister, Maggie Klein. She was an early reader of this book, but more importantly, when I was a graduate student impressed with my massive knowledge and convinced that the alcoholic was involved in a game, not a disease, she taught me otherwise. Next I'd have to mention John Daniels, because it was he who taught me about interventions, and also because he wasn't afraid to tell me that the book made him cry. Then there was Bill Makely and his wife Ethel. Without Bill's editing, I probably would have been too embarrassed to send this book to a publisher; but it was also Bill and Ethel who convinced me in the beginning that perhaps I could actually write a book.

The next person to be involved was Ann Gallagher. She not only helped type, but was also very encouraging. Early readers were Cathy Pammer, Maria Doherty, Priscilla Cross, Barb Marsh, Nancy Clough, and Ruth Etheridge, and my daughter Becky, who also did some typing. Also helping with typing and encouragement were Bev Garrett and Vicki Willey.

I received technical advice from Ken Blauw, Dick Dobbs, Rita Bobrowski, Pam Hugelan, Don Krzyzak, Mary Lou Eickleman and Bill Vlasek; but they were also helpful because they're friends who believe in me. Along that same line, I'd like to add the students and clients who all contributed to the book with their life stories and support.

My editor, Greg Pierce, made several major suggestions—as well as hundreds of minor corrections—all of which have helped the book immensely.

Finally, my wife Marsha's advice as a family therapist was invaluable. I have learned most about families, however, from living with her and our children, Becky and Bryan.

CHAPTER I

WINTER dies slowly in northern Wisconsin, and the coming of spring is more of a whisper than a pronouncement.

It's not so much the cold and snow that make people hunger for spring; it's the grey skies, and streets, and sidewalks. It's the frozen lakes and rivers. It's the lifelessness of the trees and woods. Residents search the dirty snowbanks for a trickle of melting snow, or sniff the air for that scent they have come to know. Neither sign is an assurance that winter is over; it is just the hope of things to come.

On this Sunday morning, there was the first trickle of water from the banks and the scent was in the air. Molly Brandt was on her way to church. It was much too cold to have the window open, but she cracked it a little to let the spring fragrance into the car. A southern breeze had warmed the temperature all night, so that it was warmer now than when she had gone to bed. Though it was just past dawn, she could tell already that it would be the first warm day.

Molly was a serious woman in her forties. She and her husband Hank had five children. They were all—perhaps with one exception— good kids. Molly could be attractive, but she usually wore her hair in a plain bun and never fussed much with her clothes or makeup. She was the part-time music teacher at the grade school in town, as well as the organist for the church. She was an excellent musician.

This morning she was a little more cheerful than usual, perhaps because of the scent of spring in the air and because her friend Josh was out of the hospital. He had gone in for more surgery, and though she had visited him there, it wasn't the same as seeing him around town.

Dr. Joshua Krueger was the one person in the world Molly could really talk to. He'd been the only doctor in town for as long as she could remember. Rushed as he usually was, he always seemed to find time for Molly and her problems.

They had been close ever since he helped her deal with the early death of both her parents in a car accident.

Now married with five children of her own, Molly always seemed to be going to "Dr. Josh" for something. There were school checkups and shots and bouts with the flu. Her family also seemed to have more than its share of illness and accidents.

Once, a couple of years ago, during an office visit she had talked to him about arguing with her husband, and he had asked what they fought about. She had told him "alcohol, mostly."

At first he had tried to convince her that Hank worked hard and had the right to stop for a beer or two. But then he found out how much Hank drank and how long he stayed out. He became more compassionate and listened. He had been listening ever since. Once or twice he had suggested professional help. At other times he suggested Al-Anon, a program for people with a close relationship to an alcoholic.

This shocked Molly. She wasn't sure that Hank was an alcoholic and thought professional help was too drastic a step. She continued to talk to Josh about it, however, since he was the only one she had who would listen when she needed to pour out her heart.

Josh was a quiet, even shy, man. He had never married. Rumors—and there were plenty—had it that the girl he loved had died of an unexplained illness while he was still in medical school. After that, he had buried himself in his work and seemed uncomfortable in most social situations. Over 60, with long white hair and silver bifocals, Josh was rather frail looking—especially since he had developed cancer a few years back and had undergone several operations. But he still carried himself proudly and looked distinguished.

There were only two places that Josh seemed to act confidently and openly. One was in his medical practice, where donning his white coat seemed to give him a definite role to play: the dedicated and competent physician. In his office, Josh was friendly and warm with people, and every one of his patients knew he really cared about them.

The second place Josh was free was in church. He loved music so much that when he immersed himself in it he seemed to lose most of his self-consciousness. Unfortunately, his love of music was not shared by many others in the congregation, but this did not deter Josh. In church, where he had become the hymn leader years before, he found a captive audience for his only passion. Josh was a terrible leader of song, however. Although he had a beautiful tenor voice and knew and loved the best of both the newer and the older church music, he could never transmit his enthusiasm to the rest of the congregation.

It was Josh who had spotted and developed Molly's love of music. The doctor had encouraged her as a teenager to continue with lessons and had advised her to major in music in college. When she thought of quitting in her senior year after her parents' death, it was Josh who convinced her to continue, even helping with her tuition. The two saw each other often at choir practice and would occasionally travel together to Green Bay for a concert. Josh had a great classical record collection, and he would often lend Molly the albums she could never afford to buy herself but treasured nonetheless.

Maybe it was the differences in their ages, or perhaps just their proven integrity, but their close relationship escaped the gossip so common in small communities like theirs. They would practice their hymns sometimes late into the evening, or linger over a cup of coffee at the diner, or even take day trips together without raising one eyebrow in the town.

Though Molly was delighted to see Josh chatting with Fr. Brooks when she walked into church that morning, she would never dream of hugging or even affectionately touching him. Such a display was not part of their relationship. Indeed, the entire town exhibited the effects of its German and Scandinavian roots. It wasn't that people here were cold or unfriendly; quite the contrary. There was endless socializing and neighborliness—but always at an acceptable distance.

So it was at a distance that Molly smiled when she saw her friend and said, "Welcome back, Dr. Josh."

"It's been a long winter, but I do believe spring has finally arrived," Josh, with a tilt of his head and a touch to his glasses, greeted her.

Molly and Fr. Brooks smiled at each other. They often kidded Josh about his unfading optimism.

"Oh sure, you think the old Doc's prognosis is overly optimistic," Josh declared authoritatively, "but just you wait and see. The snow and cold weather are gone until next November."

"Don't put your snowblower away just yet," Molly responded playfully. "You may just need it one more time."

"People seem late this morning," Josh said, looking around the slowly filling church.

"They're probably caught in the snow storm that developed since Molly walked in," Fr. Brooks said as he finished preparing the altar. Josh smiled, and only shook his head.

The priest began to move to the back of the church. Josh called after him "Pastor, can I have a few minutes at the beginning of the service? I want to practice a new song with the congregation."

"Sure," the priest said. "I don't feel real prepared today. Perhaps you can conduct the entire service."

"No, five minutes will be fine," Josh replied.

As the pastor continued to busy himself with preparations, Molly sat down at the organ. "How are things at home?" Josh asked.

Molly knew immediately what he meant, and her shoulders sank. "The same," she replied with discouragement evident in her voice.

"I thought so much about it while I was in the hospital," he said. "I was hoping he'd stop. He's too good a man not to see what he's doing to you and your family. I know he'll come to his senses eventually."

"Yeah," Molly said sarcastically. "And maybe the congregation will sing today, too."

It was a joke between them—but a painful joke. It was hard for the two of them who cared so deeply for music to lead a congregation where no one would sing. There were a few women in the choir and some more in church who sang softly, but Molly and Josh wanted more, much more. They wanted people to experience the richness of music as they knew and loved it.

But people here were as quiet and reserved in their worship as they were in public expressions of emotion. Some women didn't like to call attention to themselves. Some men believed that singing—especially in church—didn't fit the image of a man. Most felt that the music should be left to the pros.

"Maybe today they will," Josh said with a strange, strong conviction. Molly smiled at him, but could say no more as she needed to begin playing.

When the time arrived for the service to start, Fr. Brooks nodded to Josh to practice his new song.

Josh walked to the front of the church and Molly could almost hear the collective groan as he reached the front. They hated going over a song that just Molly and Josh were going to end up singing anyway.

"I think I'll start today by telling you a story about a friend of mine," said Josh. "He was a newly married psychiatrist who was trying to establish a practice in a new town. He was doing a lot of public speaking so people would become familiar with him. One night he was to speak on human sexuality and he was embarrassed because he really didn't feel like an expert. When his wife asked him what he would be speaking on he told her the relationship between life and a ferris wheel. That night he gave the talk.

"The next day a woman came up to his wife and told her how much she had learned from her husband's talk."

" 'Listen,' the wife told the woman, 'I know for a fact that he's only done it once. He was stuck on top for the longest time and when it finally ended, he threw up.' "

This time people did groan, but it was an affectionate laugh for they all knew Doc Josh's jokes.

"There are two parts of that story that are relevant for me today," Josh continued, "One is that I, too, am about to talk about something on which I don't consider myself an expert. That's just honesty.

"Which leads to my second lesson: both the psychiatrist and I would have been better off to be honest in the first place.

"So I'm going to be honest right now about some things that we all know anyway. First, I hate being up here. You know I don't like talking to groups. Fears are often stupid and mine are no exception. I've known many of you since I slapped your bottoms the moment you were born. You saw my face even before your mothers'. But I'm still scared to speak to you collectively. Try to figure that out!

"But I also hate being up here because this seems like confrontation between us and I hate confrontations even more than public speaking. You all know I want you to sing and I know you don't want to sing. It's like when I try to convince my patients to stop smoking and get more exercise. I usually lose those battles too." Again the congregation laughed.

"While I was in the hospital this last time I read the Bible some. One of the things I noticed about so many of the miracles Jesus performed was that he seemed to do them for people who were persistent in their asking. Today we'd call those people 'assertive.' He helped the people who wouldn't be quieted by the crowd or didn't let the apostles push them away. Occasionally, he'd even make the petitioners take part in their own cure, by washing out their eyes or ears in a river.

"I've wanted and prayed for a miracle too, but maybe I haven't done my part. Maybe I haven't been 'assertive' enough. Which reminds me of another story.

"Once there was a holy man who lived in a valley in the mountains next to a river. After a big rain the river flooded. The water kept getting deeper and he kept moving to higher ground. People would come by in boats and ask if he wanted to be rescued, but he kept saying, 'No, God will save me.' Finally, water went over the top of the mountains and the man drowned. When he went to heaven he asked God, 'Why didn't you save me?' God said, 'I tried. I kept sending you those people in boats.'"

Again the congregation laughed, for they truly loved this old man. Josh turned to Fr. Brooks, who was patiently waiting to start the regular service. "I didn't mean to go on like this," he said. "I've never felt comfortable up here before, but all of a sudden I'm enjoying myself."

"Continue," said the pastor. "This is the best homily they've heard in a long time." Again the congregation laughed.

Molly sat at the organ and wondered when was the last time such a light atmosphere had existed in the church. Josh said "Thank you, Pastor" and continued.

"Again, there are some lessons in that story for me. First, if you compare my life to those mountains, the water is just about over the top and soon I'll get a chance to ask God about my miracle. You see, they told me at the hospital I've got less than six months to live, and I just don't have much time anymore to accomplish what I've set out to do."

The congregation gasped. Molly raised one hand to her mouth and the other hand fell onto the organ keys. A discordant note immediately filled the church.

Josh, ignoring the sound, continued. "I think it's something we all knew but were afraid to talk about, but that's not my point anyway. The miracle I want is not to be saved from dying. I'm old and tired and don't need to be saved from that. What I really want is for you to sing. And I won't have to ask God why he didn't grant my miracle, because I know what he'd say." Josh was talking rapidly now, and there was no self-consciousness left. He was confident and he knew they were listening.

"He'd say 'I placed you in front of those people week after week. Why didn't you take the risk of just asking them to sing? And if they didn't do it at first, why didn't you cry out all the louder?'

"You people are my lifeboats," Josh said, "and now I'm asking you: will you sing?"

There was silence in the church. Most people had their eyes down. Molly looked straight at

Josh. "You know what's so amazing?" he continued. "I always pictured my needing to get angry in order to ask or demand that you sing, but I'm not angry now. I'm just more aware than ever how deeply I love you people. At this late date I'm still learning that love can mean other things besides acceptance. Love can mean actions too."

Josh kept going. Molly thought he had forgotten all about time or the Sunday service.

"But don't just sing for me because I'm dying," he said. "Sing for yourselves. Sing to overcome the wasted moments spent worrying about what others might think of you. Sing for your very lives so that you don't waste them as I wasted mine waiting for a miracle. Sing so you'll have the courage to make your own miracles.

"Fathers and mothers sing to show your children it's O.K. to be a little crazy. That, as a matter of fact, it's a necessity to survive in this world. Kids, sing to break out of the prison of being 'cool' or 'hot' or whatever temperature you're supposed to be these days. Sing to break free from the rules that tell us how to dress, how to act, and to whom you can or can't talk.

"But also sing to be part of my miracle. Because I have come here today, not because

I'm near death and want my hand held, but
because I'm alive and I want that to mean
something.

"I have come here today to create a miracle
and to watch it unfold. And—like the blind man
of the Bible story—I will not stop crying out
until my voice is heard. You may not think that
your singing is much of a miracle, but I promise
you, seeing you at this moment part your lips
and sing would be no less gratifying to me than
what Moses must have felt when he saw the
parting of the Red Sea.

"Please let your voices be heard. Pull out
your hymnals. I've chosen a special song for
you, called 'Be Not Afraid.' I lied. It's not new.
You've heard it before. But this time I want
you to sing it, not listen to it. I didn't know
how fitting it really was till just now. Sing your
hearts out. Don't worry, God can handle the
shock."

Josh sat down, it was over. Molly began to
play the prelude of "Be Not Afraid." She looked
at the congregation. Most seemed too stunned
to think about anything at all, much less their
own discomfort. At the proper moment she began
to sing.

"You shall cross the barren desert, but you
shall not die of thirst ..."

A few of the parishioners began to sing softly, while others looked around nervously. The soft sounds encouraged Josh, but he wasn't satisfied. From his place in the front he yelled, "That's a good start but I won't be quiet until everyone is singing."

". . . You shall wander far in safety though you do not know the way. . . ."

Several more voices joined in the singing. As Molly played she wondered how long it had been since any of these people had sung outside their showers.

But they sang, and to Dr. Joshua Krueger, they had the voices of angels. Tears poured from his sparkling eyes. He left the front and danced among them, shaking hands, picking up children and twirling with them down the aisle.

"Louder!" he shouted, and he raised his arms to direct them. Never had he shown such animation. The people began to lose some of their own inhibitions as they were caught up in his enthusiasm. They raised their voices higher, and what they lacked in quality they made up for in quantity and volume. Molly pulled out all the stops on the organ, but the people's voices continued to drown it out. Then came the antiphon.

"Be not afraid. I go before you always. . . ."

She was sure the church would soon crack
down the middle. From the shock, if not from
the sound. The people had joy on their faces.
Some were holding hands. In some of the pews
the people were actually swaying in unison to
the music. Miraculously, when the song finally
ended people actually appeared disappointed.

The church was in complete disarray. Fr.
Brooks had forgotten to start the liturgy. But
it was of little importance, since Josh immediately
yelled from the back of the church: "One more
time—from the beginning!" Molly started the
song all over again.

Josh continued to dance and sing, hug embarrassed parishioners and kiss babies. Finally,
with a child on each arm and tears in his eyes,
he appeared back at the front of church as the
song ended for the second time.

"There is no happier man on earth," he said
simply.

During the rest of the service the hymns
continued, and the congregation sang with zeal.

At the end, no one left. They all stayed to
talk—to each other and to Josh. They always
stayed to talk, but today there was a difference.
As a matter of fact there were a lot of differences.
They talked louder. They stood closer to one
another. They were even touching. Not just by

accident, but reaching over to touch a hand or an arm in mid-conversation. It was almost like a drunk, touching for blind companionship's sake on New Year's Eve. But these people were standing straight up, eyes clear and looking straight ahead.

CHAPTER II

THE first one to leave the church was Molly. She didn't stop to talk to anyone. She left as if on a mission. She went straight home. She didn't stop at the bakery as she normally did. She walked in the door, took off her coat, and went into the kitchen, where she found her oldest daughter, Bobbie.

"It's a beautiful day," Molly said. "Why don't you take the kids to the park?"

"Mom, there's still snow on the ground," Bobbie protested.

"Well, what about sledding?"

"They're tired of sledding."

"Well, then, take them for a walk!"

No more explanation was needed. It wasn't Molly's words; it was her voice. Bobbie gathered the two youngest children together and bundled them up and they were gone quickly and quietly. Molly thought of Scott and Ryan, who were still sleeping, but decided to leave them be since this time would be different: no yelling, just a quiet talk. She poured two cups of coffee and carried them to the bedroom where Hank was sleeping. She woke her husband.

"Morning," she said. "How did you sleep?"

Hank's eyes opened slowly. Although he was now almost fifty, his face still maintained a certain boyish charm. His eyes this morning, however, were clouded over like they always were after a night of drinking.

"I was doing fine till just now," he said. She handed him the coffee and sat on the edge of the bed.

"Hank, I want you to quit drinking," she blurted out.

"Does that mean I shouldn't let that coffee you brought me touch my lips?" he asked wryly.

"You know what I mean," she said.

"What brought this on all of a sudden?" he asked.

"It's not all of a sudden," she replied. "I think of it almost constantly. I've just not mentioned it for a while, that's all."

"Then why are you mentioning it now?" he asked angrily.

"I just don't want to spend the rest of my life with you passing out on the couch every night and yelling at the children," she answered.

"Well, I don't want to spend my life living with a holy roller organist either," he snapped, "but that's what I'm doing."

That startled Molly, and she retreated inside herself for a moment. She just wasn't good at this sort of thing, but she had to keep trying.

"Hank," she said, "I don't want this to be an argument. That's why I don't bring the subject up, because when I do there is always a fight and I don't want that. I just want you—all of you. I'm tired of competing with the bar and alcohol."

"Well, jump into bed here, and I'll give it my best shot," he said playfully, and pulled her by the arm.

"No, Hank. Be serious," she said, pulling her arm free and raising her voice.

"You know," he said, "that's your whole problem: you always want to be serious. You never want to have any fun, particularly in the bedroom."

"In the first place," she said, "I have too much on my mind lately to have fun. And in the second place, maybe if I had a husband who wasn't either at the bar or drunk all the time I would be interested."

"The thing I'd like to do with you now would take more than my quitting drinking to get you interested, Saint Molly!" he fired back. She knew what he was implying, and now she was angry.

"How would you know if I was interested or not?" she said, her eyes welling with tears. "You're usually too drunk to care."

Hank didn't say another word. He slowly got up and dressed and left. He didn't say where he was going. But then, she knew anyway.

Molly laid on the bed and cried. She had allowed herself once again to think that things could change. She had let herself become excited, and she knew better. Now reality came stumbling back in on her, and she was angry. Angry at Josh for making her believe she could make a difference, angry at Hank for his drinking, and angry at herself for allowing those painful feelings to take her on another rollercoaster ride.

By the time Bobbie had brought the younger children back, Molly had dried her eyes. No one asked what had happened, and she didn't volunteer any information. She was soon lost in the little obligations of the day. Scott and Ryan woke up fighting and the little ones clamored for her attention. Hank did not come home till suppertime. He was drunk, so dinner was quiet.

The day had changed from warm and sunny to cloudy with light snow. When dinner was over Hank yelled at Ryan for not shoveling the driveway, then promptly fell asleep on the couch. Molly went to bed early, a little more aware of the depression she usually called "being tired," and angry at herself for recognizing it.

CHAPTER III

It was two days before Molly saw Josh again. They always got together at midweek to go over the hymns for the Sunday service. They started as usual, each hesitating to speak what was really on his or her mind. Molly knew Josh was disappointed that she hadn't shared the joy of the past Sunday with him. After all the times they had commiserated together about the absence of singing in the services, he finally got the people to sing and she had rushed off without a word. Three days later, and she still hadn't even mentioned it!

But Molly knew she couldn't talk about it without revealing her own disappointment about Hank. So they continued to talk about next

Sunday's music with no mention of his victory. But Josh had changed. He was not as predictable as he had been, and without warning he asked "What's the matter?"

"What do you mean?" she asked. She knew it was a waste of time to dodge now that he had brought it up, but she needed time to think. He was sarcastic, another surprise.

"Oh, I don't know. The fact that I'm dying, the fact that we witnessed a miracle together— I thought you might want to comment briefly, before it was business as usual."

Molly started to cry. For the first time in their long relationship, Josh reminded her of her husband. She saw him as blaming, self-centered, and self-pitying all at the same time. Still, in spite of her anger, she immediately felt relieved, because she thought that he had given her a way out.

"I thought I was special to you," she said. "Why didn't you tell me first?"

He came to her and put his arm around her as she cried. She felt relieved. Maybe he would let her off the hook.

"You know," he said, "for my whole life what you just did would have left me apologizing all over myself. But too late I'm learning to go with my instincts: that's not what is really bothering you, is it?"

She felt betrayed, but she wasn't sure whether to be angry at herself or at Josh. She chose Josh.

"Let's just say your advice in church is not as sound as your medical advice," Molly snapped. "You should be more careful about getting people's hopes up."

Molly felt nervous and defensive. The thing she had always liked best about Josh was that he never pressed her. Now he seemed relentless. She feared she would never escape until he had read all the pages of her soul. Sure enough, he continued.

"Molly, I know and love you," he said. "You can't hide from me or push me away. But I don't have the patience I used to have, either, because I don't have the time for it now. So why not stop playing these defensive games and tell me what's going on with you?"

His voice still sounded harsh and impatient, like Hank's. But his eyes showed love, and he was only asking her how she felt. She started to laugh.

"You know, for a moment there I thought I was arguing with my husband," she said, "but I just realized you're playing my part."

He looked at her strangely.

"Never mind," she said. "I thought after last Sunday that I could go home and ask my husband to quit drinking, just like you asked the congregation to sing. But it didn't work. I knew if I started talking to you about what happened Sunday, you'd know something was wrong. I didn't want to tell you about it."

"I'm sorry about your disappointment," he said, "but please don't run from me now. If you don't need me, I sure as heck need you."

"I'm sorry, Josh. I wish I had more to give you right now."

"You know, part of your problem is you don't have death on your side the way I do." Now it was her turn to look at him strangely.

"You see, one of the reasons I had the courage to ask what I did on Sunday is because I'm dying. Death not only gave me the courage to ask, but it made it impossible for them to refuse."

"What should I do?" she asked. "Hold a gun to my head and say to my husband 'Quit drinking or else?' "

"No," he said, "but there are things other than threatening death that have power. I've asked you when we discussed this before...."

"No," she said. "I won't see a counselor."

"I don't blame you," he said. "We're a lot alike, you and I. We probably find it easier to love things that don't love back, like music.

Music sits, ever patient, waiting for us to sing or play it. Your organ never asks to be tuned, my songs never demand that I sing them a different way.

"But if your husband quits drinking he may ask you for things, and then you'll have to respond—one human being to another."

Molly didn't like the new Josh; she was sure of it now.

"You don't understand at all, do you?" she cried. "If you did, you'd know that what you say isn't true."

"Then prove it," Josh said. "Go see a counselor. If you go, and your husband still refuses help, you can truthfully tell yourself, 'I've done all I can.'"

Now she was truly hurt inside. How could anyone ask her to do more! For years she had carried the burden of raising her family single-handedly.

"You know all I've done," she said angrily. "How can you—of all people—still ask for more?"

"Did you ever stop to think that I'm encouraging you so you won't have to continue doing it all alone?"

"No," she said as she gathered her music and began walking from the room, "I never thought of it as encouragement at all."

CHAPTER IV

SHE wondered as she picked up the phone that night whether it had been Josh's intention to get her mad enough to call. If it had been, he had gotten his way. She hated herself for thinking it, but she hoped Josh lived long enough for her to tell him that the counseling had failed.

"Alcoholism Treatment, Jack Peterson speaking," a voice said at the other end.

"I'd like to speak with a counselor about my husband's drinking," said Molly.

"Would this be just for yourself, or would you be bringing your husband or family with you?"

"Just for me."

"Would you need a daytime or evening appointment?"

"Evening."

"How about Thursday at six o'clock?"

"That will be fine." Molly gave her name and wondered what she would tell the children.

When Thursday came she asked Bobbie to make dinner and watch the children and said she had a doctor's appointment. She left early and drove around until it was time. As she drove, she thought how she might explain her situation to the counselor. The more she thought, the more jumbled her mind became.

The counselor's office was at the treatment center outside of town, but she still worried that someone might see her. She parked at the back of the lot and waited until the lot was empty before leaving her car.

She was glad there was no one in the waiting room and the counselor was waiting for her. He was younger than she had expected, which made her all the more confident that this was a waste of time.

"Mrs. Brandt?" he asked as he extended his hand. She answered "Yes" as her cold wet hand found his warm one. "I'm John Peterson," he said, "but please call me Jack."

He had an open, friendly face, a shock of dark black hair that fell onto his forehead, and a way of looking straight into her eyes that Molly found disconcerting.

They went into his office and sat down. He looked at her and asked, "How can I help you?"

"As I mentioned on the phone," she said formally, "I want to talk about my husband's drinking."

"What is your problem with his drinking?" he asked matter-of-factly.

She didn't like the reference to "her" problem with Hank's drinking, but she let it pass and answered the question.

"Well, it takes him away from the family so much," she explained. "And when he is home and has been drinking, he is usually sleeping or fighting with our son or me."

"Have you spoken to him directly about it?"

"Yes, just the other day. But my doctor said that there are ways you can teach me that might have more impact."

"That's true," Jack replied. "But first we have to be sure that your husband really has a problem with chemicals. So far, you've only told me he spends a lot of time out of the house and fights with you and your son. I have two questions. One: why do you think these problems are related to alcohol? And two: can you give me specific instances when these problems occur and the role alcohol plays?"

Molly grew silent. She was only partly thinking about his questions. Another part of her was
busy resenting the fact that this counselor was
unwilling to believe that she knew the man she
had lived with for the last twenty years.

"I know these are hard questions," Jack said.
"And perhaps you feel resentful that I don't
seem ready to accept the fact that your husband
has a problem. But distrust of you is not my
reason for asking."

Molly was still silent. It was difficult for her
to be around people who seemed to know her
feelings. Especially when they were as willing to
bring them up as this man and Josh were.

"Why should I trust your judgment when
you don't seem to trust mine?" she asked.

The counselor sat back in his chair. He didn't
seem insulted or hurt, just pensive.

"Perhaps we can look at it this way," Jack
said. "You came to me for new ways to convince
your husband he has a problem. Part of that
process is collecting information you can present
to him. Think of what you're going through
now as a process of collecting information in
your mind, and also as practice in presenting it
to him."

Molly felt a little better. She still was doubtful
that this would do any good, but it was nice

to speak to someone who listened to her and whose answers made sense.

She sat and thought for a while longer. Finally she began to tell him how the relationship between Hank and her had changed over the years, and what she thought Hank's drinking had to do with it. With Jack's help she was able to identify several aspects of his drinking that—at least in her mind—made it obvious Hank was no ordinary social drinker. After a while, Jack stopped her.

"I think we have enough data to indicate we ought to proceed," he said. "We can look at more of your life at the next session if you decide you do want to go through with an intervention."

"What's an intervention?" Molly asked.

Jack sat forward in his chair and his voice softened.

"There is a good chance," he said, "that, based on what you've been telling me, your husband has the disease of alcoholism."

Molly started to protest. Jack raised his hand, stopping her.

"I know you're going to tell me he can't be an alcoholic," he said, "because he goes to work every day and is a good provider. But alcoholism has stages—like most diseases. The purpose of doing an intervention is to stop the progression of the disease before it reaches the stage where he has destroyed his life ... and his family's. But whether or not he has the disease is not as important right now as the fact that we both agree he has a problem and needs help."

Molly thought for a while and agreed.

"What do we do next?" she said.

She was ready to hear more, but what came next dampened what little enthusiasm she had.

"You need to ask your family—and maybe some others outside the family who are close to your husband—to come with you next time."

Molly's mouth dropped open.

"What do they have to do with all this?" she asked with irritation.

Jack sat back in his chair. The calm, patient look she would get to know well spread across his face.

"If in fact your husband is an alcoholic, one common symptom of the disease is denial," he said. "One person is usually not able to break through that denial. It takes either a crisis or several people telling the alcoholic the same thing at the same time to get through that wall. A family intervention combines both. The crisis for the person is seeing his loved ones all gathered together to tell him how they feel. And, the family and friends all telling him the same thing gives him a message that's difficult to deny."

"So that's what Josh meant," Molly said to herself.

"What?" Jack asked.

"Oh, nothing," Molly said. Her only thought now was to get out of there. The thought of the whole family sitting in one room, confronting her husband on his drinking, was terrifying. Once again, Jack seemed to pick up on her feelings.

"I know it must be scary to think about this," he said. "But remember, alcoholism is a progressive disease. It's going to keep getting worse, never better. The alternative is to watch your husband slowly get sicker.

"And your family will go right down with him, because we see every day that alcoholism is a family illness."

"I'll have to think about this," Molly said as a polite way of ending the conversation.

She got up abruptly and extended her hand. Jack got up slowly, trying to make eye contact, but Molly felt his gaze and looked away. He gave her a packet of information to read. "This should tell you more about how an intervention works. Call if I can answer any more questions about the process.

"Meanwhile, here's a brochure with the phone number of a local Al-Anon group. You may need some support in working through this crisis, and this group will give it to you."

Molly left quickly. She found herself taking in a deep breath of the cold night air, hoping it would cool the fire in her stomach. Instead, it sent a shiver down her back. She shook all the way home.

CHAPTER V

Once home, Molly was happy to see that Bobbie had already taken care of the dishes and gotten the little ones to bed. Hank was sleeping on the sofa. Molly didn't wake him. She just went quickly to her room to change clothes. She stuffed the packet Jack had given her in her dresser drawer.

She thought it would stay there quite awhile before she was ready to look any further into this "intervention" business.

Ryan came home while Molly was changing. He made such a racket coming in that Bobbie looked at him in surprise. He went quickly into the bathroom and threw up. Bobbie followed him in and shut the door quietly behind her.

She put her hand on his forehead and begged him to be quiet as he spit into the toilet. He just groaned, and roared again into the bowl.

Molly ran quickly, still in her robe. She was too late. Hank had already stumbled drunkenly to the bathroom. He was pounding on the door and yelling, "What's going on in there?"

"Nothing," Bobbie yelled. "Just go back to sleep, Dad."

"Don't tell me 'nothing,'" Hank shouted, and jerked open the door.

"What's the matter with you?" he asked Ryan.

"Mush haff da flu," Ryan mumbled as he stumbled to his feet, wiping his mouth.

"You're drunk!" his father answered.

"Takes one to know one!" Ryan replied sullenly.

Hank was on Ryan in a second and had the boy by the scruff of the neck. The father had had years of practice maneuvering while drunk—a technique at which his young son was not yet accomplished. Ryan was no match for him, and Hank soon had his son's face in his own vomit in the toilet bowl.

Bobbie and Molly rushed to separate them.

"Stop! You'll kill him," they both shouted at once.

"He'll only wish he was dead," Hank grunted. When he let the boy's head up, Ryan was coughing and his face was covered with vomit. Hank's jaw was set. Molly quickly stepped between them with a wash cloth. She looked at Ryan as she wiped his face.

Instinctively, she knew the best way out of this was to support her husband.

"What's the matter with you?" she scolded Ryan.

"I'll take care of him and get him to bed," she said to her husband over her shoulder. "We'll decide on a punishment for him in the morning." She held her breath as she continued to clean Ryan's face.

She breathed again when Hank turned to stumble out of the bathroom.

He turned in the doorway and said, "You haven't heard the last of this, young man!" But he continued out of the room.

Molly sighed. Bobbie followed her father.

Knowing the dance steps to relieve the crisis, the teenager simply agreed as her father mumbled about the disrespectful kids who don't appreciate all that's been done for them.

Molly and Bobbie finally got everyone to bed. They sat quietly for a while in the living room, as if to catch their breath. In their tiredness they didn't speak, just stared at the empty space in front of their faces.

That was the closest Molly would come to sleep that night. She lay all night on the living room couch, not wanting to be next to her husband. She kept thinking about the words the counselor had used: "progressive family disease." Even if it didn't get worse, even if he was the only one with the problem, she didn't want herself or her family subjected to it anymore.

In the morning, she woke Bobbie first.

"I know you must be tired, but I need your help. Get the little ones ready for school. I'll try to keep Dad away from Ryan."

Bobbie nodded in agreement and quickly rose to get dressed. Molly went next to Ryan's room. She spoke sternly.

"Ryan, get up for school."

"I'm sick, Mom," was his reply.

Now she spoke with fire: "Damn right you're sick. I hope you're as sick as a dog, but if you think you're skipping school, you're crazy."

The boy's feet were quickly on the floor.

Molly then went to wake her husband.

"I'm awake," he said. "You must have gotten up early."

"Yes," she said sharply.

"Boy, you're in a foul mood," said Hank. "What's the matter?"

Molly knew immediately that her husband had no recollection of what had happened the night before.

"I didn't sleep well," she said. She left the room not sure if she was relieved or angry.

When Ryan saw Hank in the hall a minute later, he quickly lowered his eyes.

"Can't you even say good morning?" his father yelled.

"Good morning," Ryan said quietly, trying not to draw any attention to himself.

At the breakfast table Paul, the youngest son, complained of bad dreams. Sally, the youngest of all, missed her mouth with her oatmeal. Everyone laughed, so she did it again. Finally, when they had all left, Molly called the school to say she was sick and would not be in that day. She went to her room and pulled the packet of material from her dresser drawer. She had not expected to look at it so soon.

She first read the material that described the intervention process. It spoke of how the family presents the dependent person with the reality of his or her chemical use.

She read that there would be four sessions. The first would be assessment and education. She and her family would have to talk again with Jack and further convince him that Hank had a problem. They would be taught in the first session how to prepare specific data. That meant they would need to think about specific instances when Hank drank and how it affected them.

In the second session, they'd see a film about an intervention and go over their data with Jack.

The third session, they'd role play doing their intervention. They would have to decide on the order in which people would make their presentations and where they would sit. Finally would come the intervention itself, where they would sit with Hank and present their case to him.

This all seemed so impossible. She was sure the kids would dislike talking and planning without their father knowing it. She was also sure Hank would have a fit if he walked into a room and they were all sitting there. He would never tolerate listening to the children confront him about his drinking, and he would really be upset if she brought in anyone from outside the family.

She read on. She was supposed to approach the intervention with love and concern and be nonjudgmental. At the moment, though, she wasn't feeling that much love and concern and she felt very judgmental.

When presenting her data to Hank, she would have to talk about how she felt. She had spent most of her married life trying to forget how she felt, and now she was supposed to talk about it.

At the end of the intervention, they were supposed to give Hank options about treatment. How did she know what options to suggest when she herself wasn't sure? There was only one thing that moved her toward the phone, and that was her pain. She was afraid for Hank, but most of all worried about her children. She called the treatment center.

"I wasn't so sure I'd hear from you, especially so soon," Jack said.

"I have some more questions," she said. "Do you have time to see me today?" They made an appointment for later that morning.

CHAPTER VI

MOLLY hoped that Jack would again be waiting when she arrived at the treatment center, but he wasn't. This time she had to sit and wait for him. It was hard for her, because she was so tired of the thoughts that seemed to constantly run through her mind no matter what she did: the thought that her husband might be an alcoholic; the idea that the whole family was sick. These were too much for her today.

But the scene from the night before continued to haunt her: her teenage son drinking; her husband's angry reaction, and then his remembering nothing the next day; she herself awake that whole night, then calling in sick the next day. One thing certainly was true: all in the family were affected by Hank's drinking.

Jack finally emerged from his office, and she was glad to see him. It amazed her that this person she had only seen once before affected her so strongly, but he did. It wasn't what he said, but the way he listened and seemed to understand.

"Hi!" he said as he came over to shake her hand.

"Hi!" she repeated, and followed him into the office.

"What brings you back so soon?" he asked.

"Well," Molly said, "I had fully intended when I left last night to never return, but something happened at home that changed my mind. It made me think that maybe some of the things you said had some truth to them." She related the events of the night before.

"Well," said Jack, "There is no perfect screening test for the disease, but I look for certain clues or symptoms. You describe several things from last night that lead me to believe that a problem exists. Hank's not remembering is an example of what we call a blackout—a loss of memory. The fact that his behavior is very different when he's drinking and that his drinking is obviously getting in the way of his functioning in the family are symptoms of the disease. And all that's from just one incident."

"I was afraid you'd say that," Molly said, "because that leads me to my next question. Is there any way for my husband to get help other than the way you started to describe last night?"

Jack sat back in his chair. "Sure," he said. "There are lots of ways. He may kill someone while driving drunk. He may lose his job as a result of his drinking and quit because of that. You could threaten to divorce him, or one of the children could run away. But it usually takes some crisis that he can relate directly to his drinking to get him to stop. We call this 'hitting bottom.' It's the point at which the alcoholic finally says, 'I've had enough; I've got to quit.' "

"But I don't want any of those things to happen," Molly said. "Besides, he works for his brother and he's a great worker. And things would have to get much worse before I'd even consider separation."

"That's just it," Jack said. "An intervention is designed to 'raise his bottom' as we describe it—to set up a crisis that, in the long run, doesn't hurt him or anyone else, yet helps him decide to quit drinking."

"So what do we do, sit around and threaten him?"

"No, that's the beauty of the way we do interventions here. They work through love, not power."

"Tell me exactly how it works."

"Well, first you must get your family, and perhaps a close friend or relative—the brother he works for, for instance—to agree to gather together and tell your husband how his drinking has affected them. Then each one will tell Hank that they love him and want him to get help. If he agrees, he'll go right into one of our programs here."

"It sounds so easy the way you describe it; what if some of these people won't be involved?"

"That's quite possible. Often the people around the alcoholic have as much denial as the alcoholic himself. But it is important for the success of the intervention that at least four, and preferably five, are willing to participate."

A sudden thought entered Molly's mind.

"What if it doesn't work?" she asked anxiously. "What if all our honesty just makes him angry?"

"Well, there are no guarantees," Jack said, "but we have a good track record. Honesty and risk don't offer any promises, just possibilities and hope. The alternative, though, is to go home and pretend last night didn't happen. That means you live a lie and teach your children to live a lie and ignore reality.

"They will walk around in their private world, distrusting what they see. They will learn not to talk, not to trust, and not to feel.

"Let's not even take last night. When was the last time you or any of your children said 'Dad, why are you so often drunk at the dinner table? Why do you fall asleep on the couch every night? Why does everyone ignore it when you stumble, or when you talk funny?'

"Everyone has learned to pretend those things aren't happening. Is that how you want your children to go through their life, Molly?

"I'll bet they've seen you crying after a fight. They may have found the courage to ask, 'Mommy, why are you crying?' You got angry at them and said 'I'm not crying' or 'I'm not angry.' You're teaching them not only to mistrust their own perceptions, but also that feelings should be denied at all costs."

Molly was shocked and surprised. Was this guy a mouse in her living room? How did he know these things went on in her family?

Whatever the case, when Molly had to choose between honesty and the alternative just presented by Jack, the answer was obvious.

"And even if your husband doesn't agree to go into treatment," said Jack, "through the intervention I think you'll all learn new ways of dealing with your husband's drinking that will help you and your family."

Molly sighed. Maybe she'd better check out Al-Anon for some support.

CHAPTER VII

MOLLY told herself to wait until the weekend, when Scott would be home from college, but what she really needed was the time to rehearse what she would say and build up her own courage.

She thought the best move would be to take the time to speak to Hank's brother, Ken. She knew that would also help build up her courage. Ken and she had been friends since the day they had met. She knew he loved his brother, and, though they had never talked about it, she knew that he, too, was concerned about Hank's drinking. That's how it was with them: they knew each other's heart without it being spoken.

That's why she knew also where the problem would be in getting Ken involved. Ken had always spent a lot of time with them before he was married. He was Hank's younger brother. He had stayed single a long time, which was one reason he could take the risk of starting his own construction company. He had wanted Hank to go in with him, but by that time Scott had been born and Bobbie was on the way. So Ken went it alone.

Ken was honest and reliable. His business had flourished because people liked him and could count on him. Soon Hank started to work for him as his foreman and that helped, too, because Hank was a better boss. Though the men liked Ken, they often took advantage of him. Hank let no one take advantage of himself or his brother.

But eventually Ken had gotten married and, as often happens, this kind and generous man married a selfish woman.

"Maybe that's not fair to her," Molly thought, "because Martha does love Ken. She just does it in a possessive and domineering way. She really doesn't want to share Ken with anyone."

At any rate, Molly knew that the only way to get Ken into the intervention was as a package deal: Ken and Martha.

So Molly called Martha and asked if she might come over to visit them that evening. She asked Martha to tell Ken not to mention anything to Hank, and that she would explain why that evening. Martha sounded confused, but agreed.

Molly went to their house after dinner, telling her family she had to practice the organ at church. When she arrived, Ken and Martha had finished eating and were having coffee in their living room. She joined them and tried to make pleasant conversation, but she could see their minds were on why she had really come.

"I know," Molly said, "you must be wondering why I'm here and why I asked you not to tell Hank. I'll get right to the point. I think Hank's drinking has gotten out of hand and I'm seeing a counselor about it. He says the best way for us to help Hank is to get together family and friends who care about him and to have all of them confront him together. Then all of them will ask him to get help. I'm here to ask you if you two would help me with this."

Ken opened his mouth first, but Martha's words came out faster. Her words dripped with concern, none of which Molly believed.

"Molly, you poor dear," Martha said, "I knew that your life was hard living with that

man, but do you think it would help if we were
there? Hank and I have never been very close,
and Ken would risk losing a brother and a good
employee if this doesn't work."

"I know I'm asking a lot," Molly said, "but
there is no other person I'd dare turn to with
this."

This time, Ken won and got his words out
first. And he spoke with more force than Molly
had heard him use before with his wife.

"We would be glad to help, Molly."

He turned to Martha. "But dear, you're right
about you and Hank not being close. I think
I should go alone."

Molly fought back the smile on her face as
she spoke.

"Thanks, Ken!"

Martha spoke through a tight smile: "Well,
Ken, if you think it best. . . . But maybe we
should discuss it tonight and call you in the
morning, Molly."

Molly had a sinking feeling. Leaving Ken to
discuss anything with Martha scared her; she
knew who would be doing the discussing. But
Ken quickly quieted her fears.

"We'll discuss whether it's better for one or
both of us to come," he said, "but you can
count on the fact that I will be with you for
sure and we'll both be there in spirit."

Martha's eyes looked at Ken in disbelief, but her voice said "Of course you can count on us."

"Thanks again!" Molly said. "Now I'd better be going. I don't want Hank to get suspicious. I told him I was going to practice the organ."

She stopped with her hand on the door knob.

"I hate this lying," she said in a helpless voice. Then she went on, in a stronger vein. "I haven't even asked the kids yet, but I'm sure they'll go along with it. I'll ask them this weekend when Scott is home."

As Molly drove home she thought, "How I'd like to be a little mouse inside Ken and Martha's house." She knew Martha would have a few things to say. But she felt confident now that Ken would not back down. She knew now also that she could talk to them about the problem no matter how things worked out in the intervention. She was beginning to see what Jack meant about how things would change even if Hank didn't quit drinking after the intervention.

She thought about Josh and about how what he had done was making an impact not only on her life now but perhaps on Ken and Martha's as well. She thought about how she had left him so abruptly a few days before. Perhaps she should stop by and apologize. Then she looked at her watch and decided against it. She didn't want Hank asking questions just yet.

Jack had told her to tell Hank she was going to an addictions counselor, but she didn't want to do that now. She was sure he'd object, and, though she felt stronger every day, she didn't feel ready to stand up to him yet.

CHAPTER VIII

On Sunday morning, Molly went to church early as usual. She was hoping to see Josh, but Fr. Brooks told her he was back in the hospital. Without Josh there the people still sang, but their voices were much quieter, much less strong.

Fr. Brooks went through the first part of the service with his usual dull efficiency. Molly was praying for strength to continue with this intervention. It was scary to think of talking to the children—and that was nothing compared to facing Hank. She needed inspiration, but she didn't expect to get it from her pastor.

He was a young man, but old for his years. In many ways, he's perfect for this town and this congregation, Molly often thought. The priest was an intellectual who had studied at the University of Chicago. He had been sent to this parish by the bishop for some "pastoral experience" before he joined the faculty at the seminary.

As he began his sermon, the priest said quietly that he had noticed that the people were singing more softly this morning and that a part of him was glad about that. Molly sank down in her seat at the organ. She didn't want to hear more about singing. She started to tune out and turn inside for strength.

"All my life," Fr. Brooks said, "I have said to myself that what we do doesn't make any difference. It really doesn't matter what happens on this earth, because we are only here for a brief moment. I was never quite sure if my religion made me that way, or if I was taken with religion and became a clergyman because it fit so well with what I believed anyway. 'It doesn't make any difference,' I said to myself over and over. 'It doesn't matter if I'm a pastor or a professor or a bishop.'

"When I'd see people who seemed to need help, I'd say to myself 'It doesn't matter what I do or don't do. It will all work out according to God's plan. God will get them the help they need. And even if he doesn't, it doesn't matter because they will probably learn something from their misfortune.'

"Then, last Sunday, I was here when Josh asked you to sing. I had a violent reaction in my stomach. I'm not sure what was happening inside of me, but I know it made me uncomfortable. That's why there is a part of me that's glad to hear things returning to normal, because I don't like feeling uncomfortable. As a matter of fact, I don't like feeling at all."

Molly sat up straight on her bench. "As all of you know by now, I like to think," said the pastor, "and I don't like my thinking interrupted or even stimulated by affairs of the earth. I have all I can do to wonder about the heavens without being bogged down with the trivial human conditions on earth. Last Sunday I was jolted into humanness, a new and mysterious world that I know less about than the heavens. All of a sudden, when I heard Josh talk, it mattered to me that you sang. When I saw people talking, laughing and hugging after church I was trembling. What he did seemed to make a difference.

"I thought for a long time about why that was so frightening to me. I came up with three reasons. One, I'm scared to death of closeness. Two, I'm scared to death of feeling. And three,

I'm scared to death of the presence of God, who was more evident to me here last Sunday than he has ever been in my years of thinking."

Molly couldn't believe her ears. Neither could most of the congregation.

"So I'm going to ask—no, plead—with you," said the priest, "to continue to sing and to ignore the part of me that likes things the way they were. I want you to sing for God, because I hope he likes being present in the way that he was last Sunday. I want you to sing for yourselves, because I think we all need to feel alive. I want you to sing for Josh so that he can hear you in his hospital bed, and I believe he can. But most of all, although it may be selfish, I want you to sing for me. Because even though it scares me to death I want to feel again, and I know I need you and your voices for that."

Then, right there on the pulpit, just for a moment, he cried. Then he caught himself.

Molly never made it inside herself for inspiration. Fr. Brooks had provided all the inspiration she needed. She thought about herself and her family. She wondered when the last time was that they had expressed feelings, other than anger, to each other. There seemed to be an unspoken rule in the family that didn't allow feeling. But now she felt like changing that and she believed she could make a difference.

For two Sundays in a row now, two usually quiet men of this community had given her a gift she thought she might never be able to repay. But she could play the organ, and they were going to hear it like never before. She announced the next hymn, and played the organ with her body and soul. They both showed through.

It was a joy to play the organ and to get lost in the music and the enthusiasm. It gave her even more of the strength she needed to go home and talk to her family. But she knew they'd still be asleep, so she waited around afterwards to speak with some of the parishioners. She found out that Josh was indeed in the hospital, but was resting comfortably. For a brief moment she thought about what would happen if she never saw him again but quickly pushed it from her mind. She needed all her energy to be focused on her family right now.

She went home and made breakfast and thought of ways to keep all the children home while Hank went to "church." It was the family joke that his service started when the bars opened on Sunday. They had breakfast in the usual manner, and after it was finished she announced that the house needed cleaning and all the children were to stay and help. There were groans, but they all stayed—even Scott. Hank soon left, grumbling that "it was about time somebody did something around this house besides me."

As his car pulled out of the driveway, Molly called everyone into the living room and asked them to sit.

"What's up?" Bobbie asked. Molly sat quietly for a moment.

"I think it is time that we talk about a few things as a family," she said.

"But Dad's not here," Ryan quickly pointed out. "Isn't he part of the family?"

"Yes," Molly answered, "but he's what I want to talk about. I think your father has a drinking problem and needs our help to face up to it."

"Mom," Bobbie said, "do you really think Paul and Sally should be involved in this conversation?"

"I'm not sure any of us should be. Dad isn't even here to defend himself," Scott said.

Molly held up her hands and the room was quiet. "In the first place," she told them, "it affects all of us, so I think we all need to be involved. In the second place, Dad will have plenty of time to 'defend himself,' if he feels we are attacking him. But first we need to learn the proper way of telling him how we feel about his drinking."

"And how we going to learn that, Mom?" Ryan asked sarcastically. "Are you going to teach it to us in a song?"

"Don't be a smart ass," Scott growled.

"I wouldn't dare act like you!" Ryan fired back. The two boys glared at one another.

"Why don't both of you pay attention to something besides your petty fights?" Bobbie snapped.

"All right! All of you stop," Molly said firmly. "We would learn how by going to a counselor."

They all sat for a moment frozen. Scott was the first to break the silence.

"That's ridiculous," he said.

"Why do you say that, Scott?" Molly asked.

"In the first place, Dad may drink a little too much," he announced, "but he doesn't have a 'problem' as you call it. Second, even if he did, he can take care of it himself and doesn't need us and some counselor sticking our collective nose into his business."

"You haven't been around lately, Scott," Bobbie said. "Daddy hardly ever comes home sober, and he doesn't even remember the things he says and does. The other night he had a big fight with Ryan and the next morning he acted like nothing had happened."

"The problem is, without me around Dad has no reason to come home sober," Scott said.

"The rest of you are just one big disappointment to him."

"My, aren't we Mister Wonderful," Ryan said sarcastically again. "Dad's big hero son that none of the rest of us can hold a candle to. But then who would want to. The glare from your ego would blind us! No wonder you don't want to do this thing with Dad. You don't want to tarnish your image by saying anything that might offend your precious father."

Scott glared at Ryan. He looked down at him. He looked down in all ways. He was older, bigger, smarter, even a better athlete. He truly was his father's pride and joy, and he knew it.

"Yes," he said to Ryan, "and you needn't worry, 'cause your image is so far in the sewer you couldn't resurrect it with a diving bell."

With that, Ryan flew across the room at Scott. One quick sideways move and a slight shove from Scott, however, and Ryan flew past, scraping his face on the carpet.

"Stop it!" Molly shouted, as Bobbie rushed to help pick up Ryan and keep him away from Scott. "I have enough problems right now dealing with your father without worrying whether you two are going to kill each other."

"Oh, Ma!" Scott said. "No one is going to kill anybody, and if you worry about Dad it's your own fault. There is nothing to worry about. He's fine."

"That's what I hate about you so much," Ryan shouted. "You walk around with your head in the clouds. You have no idea what it's like to be a mere human being like the rest of us. For you life is one big walk in the park, and nothing should bother anyone."

Molly was getting tired. She had not expected the children to be such a problem. She realized that she didn't know them as well as she thought she did. Perhaps she'd been too busy thinking about Hank to notice them.

"Look at all the problems this is causing," Bobbie said. "Maybe we'd be better off leaving well enough alone."

"But that's the problem: it's not 'well enough,'" Molly insisted. "This discussion isn't what is causing the problem. It's all the times we all have decided to leave well enough alone to the point where we don't know what 'well' is anymore."

"I'm going to go through with this, and I have already asked Uncle Ken and Aunt Martha to help and they've agreed. Now which of you is going to join me?"

The room grew silent. The children all looked shocked. Scott was again the first to speak.

"You mean to tell me that you included Dad's boss in on this crazy scheme of yours?" he demanded.

"Let me inform you that he is first and foremost your father's brother," said Molly.

"But Mom," Bobbie chimed in, "Dad's not going to like this in the first place, but he will really be mad if we ask outsiders."

"I like Uncle Ken," Sally added.

Paul raised his hand as if he were in school, and just as in school, no one seemed to notice.

"Dad also knows how to control all of us, and that's why we need outside help," said Molly. "I don't want to live my life in fear anymore, and I don't want you children to, either. It's time we started acting instead of reacting."

"Where are you learning all these cute little phrases from, Mom?" Scott sneered. "From the same counselor who is teaching you to make a mess of this family?"

Molly looked sharply at Scott.

"If that's the way they teach you to talk to your parents in college, young man, then you can just go back there and stay. I don't have to put up with that."

Scott stood up and said, "And I don't have to put up with this nonsense either!" And he walked out.

Molly took a quick breath. It was rare for her to have a fight with Scott. In fact, he usually related mostly to his father. If it had been the other way around—if she had the problem—she knew he would have stayed with Hank. But she couldn't worry about that now.

"If anyone else wants to leave this room and not go through with this, now is the time," Molly said. "I'll try not to hold it against you."

No one else left.

"I can't guarantee I'll go through with this, but I'll at least stay and find out more about it," Bobbie said.

"I'll go," Ryan said. "It'll be nice to have somebody else be the center of attention around here besides me."

"I'll go if you want me to," Sally said.

Paul was quiet. But then, Paul was always quiet. Molly was just about to tell them the time and date of the first meeting when he said, "I'll go."

CHAPTER IX

T HOUGH she was usually warm and friendly to them, when Bobbie saw Ken and Martha in the waiting room of the treatment center that Tuesday night she gave them a look that made it clear they should keep their distance. She sat on a chair in a corner of the lobby and never looked up. Molly gave her in-laws both a hug and thanked them for coming. Ryan gave his usual grunt and sat next to Bobbie. Sally bounced into the room and jumped on her Uncle Ken. Paul slipped in behind her and sat off by himself.

Then they all sat in nervous silence, waiting for Jack to come out of his office. When he finally emerged, the room almost crackled with tension, but, as usual, Jack was soft-spoken and friendly. His voice sounded almost apologetic as he introduced himself to each of the family members. When he got to Paul, Jack asked him his name as he extended his hand in a greeting. Paul looked at it in shock and disbelief while Jack stood there frozen. Sally laughed.

"That's called a hand, Paul," she said, "and when someone puts it in front of you, you're supposed to grab it and shake it like this."

She stepped in front of Paul and shook Jack's hand. She sounded as if she were talking to a foreigner who didn't understand the custom. It made everyone laugh as they walked into the office. But by the time each person had found a chair, their smiles had faded and they were serious again. Molly looked around the room into each face. She smiled at each person who was willing to look at her, but most—except for Martha—looked at the floor.

Jack broke the ice.

"Molly, I'd like to know what you told the family to get them to come," he asked.

"Well, basically I said that I thought Hank's drinking had gotten out of hand and that he needed help with it," Molly explained. "I said I didn't think he would get that help on his own and that we needed to convince him that he needed it."

"That's good," said Jack. "Now here's what I would like to do here tonight. First, I want to answer your questions about the process. Then I want you to convince me that Hank has a problem.

"If you can convince me that Hank needs help, then I'll send you home to write down the experiences you can remember—your experiences with his drinking. When you come back, we'll do some planning, and I'll show you a film of another family very much like yours doing an intervention. Finally, on the night before the actual intervention, we'll go through a practice—a dress rehearsal, sort of.

"I always schedule the intervention for a morning, because I'll only do this if the person is sober. It also helps us, since it usually takes a while every day for most of us to get our defenses firmly in place, and that means we'll be more honest and have a better chance of making an impression on Hank." He looked around the room.

"Any questions?"

"Yes," Martha said. "Can you do the intervention on a Saturday? My husband and Hank work from Monday through Friday."

"I don't usually work on Saturday and I don't like doing interventions then. If working people don't have to get up on Saturday, they stay out late drinking on Friday night—and they may still be drunk on Saturday when we're trying to communicate with them."

"That's no problem," Ken said. "I can take time off, and since I'm Hank's boss, he won't have any trouble either."

Molly saw Martha's face harden, but she remained quiet.

"Speaking of work," Ken continued, "Hank is the best worker I've got. He can work longer and harder that I can. Can he really have a drinking problem if it doesn't affect his job?"

"Well," Jack said, "often a man's job is the last thing to be affected, because it's so important to him. It gives him self-respect. A person may lose his house and family, but he makes sure he has a good work record for as long as he possibly can."

"Do you think my Dad is an alcoholic?" Ryan asked. The people in the room squirmed a little, but Jack remained calm.

"Well, from some of the things your Mom has told me, I think that's a possibility," Jack responded. "But that's one of the main reasons you're here now: to determine if your father has a problem. I still need to be convinced."

"I feel as though I'm stabbing him in the back talking about him this way," Bobbie said.

"It may seem that way now," said Jack, "but when your father walks in here, if he does, you will have a chance to be more open and direct with him than you ever have before in your life. And it's important for you to know that you are here out of love, not to hurt or get even. And if you're not, he'll see through it right away, and it won't work."

"But why do we have to do it this way?" Bobbie asked. "It seems so mean!"

Jack looked at the other faces in the room, and he could see the same questioning feeling in them all.

"All right, let me explain," he said. "If your dad has a problem with drinking, one of the biggest symptoms of that problem is that he doesn't believe that a problem exists in the first place. It's called 'denial' and it's part of having what we call the disease of alcoholism, just like having a runny nose is part of having a cold.

"It usually takes some sort of a crisis—some terrible result of drinking, like hurting someone in an auto accident, or losing a job—to break through that denial and show the alcoholic that he really has a problem. What we're trying to do is create a controlled crisis to help your father realize he has a problem—something that will show him what has happened to him without hurting anyone or costing him his job ... or his family."

He paused, and looked around at the solemn faces surrounding him.

"But before I answer any more of your questions, suppose you answer some of mine," said Jack. "Maybe we'll decide you don't really need to be here. What makes you think Hank has a problem?"

Ken spoke first, slowly and thoughtfully.

"When I first started the business, Hank and I would stop every night after work at a bar in town. The business was new, and it was fun and exciting to talk over our plans for the future. I guess I grew up with a notion that it would be fun to stop after work and have a beer with the guys. Our parents didn't drink at all, so I suppose drinking for both of us was sort of a forbidden fruit.

"At first I didn't notice—or care—how late it got, because I had no place in particular to go. Then I began to date Martha, and I noticed for the first time that once Hank started to drink, he didn't want to stop. I'd go in for a beer or two, then want to leave, but Hank would try to talk me into one more beer and then one more. If I asserted myself and said I had a date, he'd start making cracks about caring more about Martha than about him or the business. But after a while I realized that Hank cared more about drinking than about me and just wanted someone to drink with. Drinking meant more to him than my company.

"Now I'm here because I want a relationship again with my brother. I'm sure he blames Martha for the fact that we're not as close as we once were, but I feel it's the alcohol that has come between us."

"Very good," Jack said. Then he turned to Martha.

"What about you, Martha? Why are you here?"

"Mostly, I'm here for Ken," Martha said. "I know he'd like to be close to his brother, and misses the relationship they had. I never suspected the alcohol. I just thought Hank was loud and obnoxious by nature."

Molly looked over at Bobbie. She knew that Bobbie was not wild about her Aunt Martha under any circumstances. That comment wasn't going to help their relationship. Bobbie looked sharply at Martha, but said nothing.

"It's hard for me to know how alcohol affects Hank," Martha continued, "because I've rarely seen him not drinking. I guess the time I'm most upset about, though, was at our wedding when he got up to make a toast. He not only slurred his words, but he made several lewd comments about our wedding night."

"How did you feel about that?" Jack asked.

"I was embarrassed and humiliated," Martha said with irritation in her voice.

"You may think it strange that I ask you that," Jack said, "but one of the most important things for you to do when we actually do this intervention is to tell Hank exactly how you feel. Hearing you express the feelings he has caused in you—all of you—will help more than anything else to break through Hank's denial."

Jack turned to Molly next.

"What can you tell me that might convince me that Hank has a problem?"

Molly sat for a moment. At this point she was concerned about the children. How would they feel toward their father after hearing all of this?

"First, let me say that Hank has always been a good and loyal husband, father, and provider. He has never run around with other women, he has never hurt me or the children, and we have never gone hungry because of his drinking. Doing this would be a lot easier if he had. But I think the thing that hurts me the worst is what he seems to have lost because of his drinking.

"Hank never went to college, but he was intelligent. Even though I did go to college, I usually felt inferior to him in a discussion. He liked to read, and we would talk for hours about books we had both read."

Paul and Sally looked at their mother as if she was discussing a man they didn't know. Molly looked back at them and smiled for a moment, but then tears filled her eyes.

"See, that is what is so sad." She put her arms around her two youngest children's shoulders as they sat on each side of her. "You two have never known that man. It's like he's a different person now. It's like there is a vacuum in his head. He says things and doesn't remember them."

"That's what I hate the worst," blurted Ryan. "That's where most of our fights come from. He tells me I can do something, then when I do it he yells at me because he doesn't remember giving me permission."

"What about you, Bobbie?" Jack asked.

Bobbie looked down at the floor. "Well, I guess dinner time is the worst for me, especially Sunday dinners. I remember a time when my dad stayed home on Sunday. We would sometimes take walks or go fishing. Or Scott and Dad would watch a ballgame on T.V. On Sunday

Mom had more time to cook, and we had nice meals that were pleasant. Now Dad is usually drunk when he comes home, and any little thing makes him real angry. So we all sit on pins and needles afraid to say or do the wrong thing. I'm so nervous I don't want to eat, but I know if I don't he'll yell about that."

"When I spill my milk he yells," Sally added.

"Not like he'd yell at me if I did it," Ryan added quickly. "When he yells at you he's smiling, for God's sake."

Everyone looked at Sally's cute face and smiled.

"What about you, Paul?" Jack asked.

"My dad doesn't say much to me," was all Paul could say.

"Maybe that's a problem," Jack said.

Paul looked at him curiously.

"O.K.," Jack interrupted. "I think we've heard enough facts to tell us we should continue with this."

He stood up and gazed at them, like a teacher in front of a class.

"From what you've all said I've gathered that alcohol affects Hank's most primary relationships—his family. I've learned that once he starts to drink he can't stop and that his drinking has gotten worse over time. Finally, I've learned that he has memory lapses related to alcohol.

"That is enough to convince me that he has a problem, that he suffers from alcoholism." He looked into each of the faces before him.

"But it's not nearly enough to convince Hank," Jack concluded. "To convince Hank that he has a problem we need two things. One, we need specific things he did—incidents where his behavior was affected by alcohol—which in turn affected you. He needs to know about the promises he has broken, the thoughtless things he did or said while drinking, and the things he didn't do because of drinking. Second, he needs to know how that made you feel.

"I want you each to go home and think about these things and write them down. Then I want you to bring them with you the next time we meet. You can set up a meeting time with the receptionist outside. See you then."

They filed out of the office quietly after saying their own goodnights to Jack. They made an appointment for the following week. Ken and Martha left in their car and Molly and the children in theirs. They didn't talk much on the way home. Molly asked the children how they had liked Jack. Together they murmured "Fine," but their lack of enthusiasm was heavy in the dark car.

CHAPTER X

THAT night, Bobbie helped get the little ones to bed as usual, then sat quietly in the living room with Molly. Molly knew there was a lot on her mind and gave her daughter time to think, but finally could take it no longer.

"What's up?" Molly asked.

"Mom, I don't think I can go through with this," she said. She looked relieved to have said it. Molly wasn't surprised.

Molly didn't want to speak too quickly. Since her decision to take this step had been made, it seemed all she had done was sort through alternatives. On the one hand she knew her daughter was important to the intervention, yet she also knew it was time for everyone in the family to start having choices. For their whole lives, the children had been stuck in boxes: Scott was the good one; Ryan was the bad one; Sally was the funny one; Paul was the quiet one. Then there was Bobbie; she was the helpful one.

Molly knew all she had to do was say "The children need you" and Bobbie would feel bound to comply. It was very difficult for Molly not to say it. But she didn't. She forced herself to look surprised and say, "Oh. Why not?"

Bobbie took a deep breath.

"It's been hard for me these last few years to maintain any kind of respect for Daddy," Bobby explained. "I've been embarrassed so many times by things he has done and said. He's never touched me, but when he's drunk, sometimes he says things to me that make me feel like he's talking to a woman at the bar he's just left. Then the next day I see him and sometimes he looks right past me and I know he doesn't remember. Other times he sees me and looks like he wants to crawl into a hole. That's what I'd have to say if I were there, and I just can't do that in front of Ken and Martha and the counselor."

At that moment, Molly hated the world and everyone in it, including the God who had created it. She looked at her lovely young daughter. She wondered if in her whole life Bobbie had ever done anything wrong. It seemed she was born fully grown and had probably worried about causing her mother pain when she had pushed her way out into the world. What had Bobbie ever done to cause anyone pain? Yet here she was, going through this torture. Molly knew the intervention was the only way to end this agony, but she didn't have the heart to see her daughter suffer any more. She went to Bobbie and sat with her. Mother and daughter hugged one another as Bobbie sobbed and tears rolled down Molly's cheeks.

"You've done enough for this family already," Molly said. "Giving up your youth is already too high a price. You can skip the intervention. But I'm going to continue so you'll never have to suffer like this again."

"Thank you, Mom," Bobbie whispered, almost out of breath. "And I'm sorry." Molly withdrew from the hug and grabbed her daughter firmly by the shoulders. She looked into Bobbie's sad eyes, still full of tears.

"You have nothing to apologize for," Molly said forcefully. "You've done nothing wrong and don't ever think that you have."

Shortly after they both went to bed. Molly lay awake and wondered how the intervention was ever going to be successful if she kept losing important people. Bobbie lay in bed with her mother's words running through her mind: "Your youth is enough of a sacrifice." It didn't seem to fit with what she had told her mother. But the confusion and exhaustion of the day finally got to Bobbie, and she fell asleep. Molly never did. Finally, despairing of ever falling asleep, she got up to write down the details Jack had asked for.

At first, it was hard for her. She had spent so many years defending Hank, it seemed impossible now for her to turn around and begin to accuse him—even in spite of what her daughter had just told her. Her first instinct was to excuse him.

She was convinced that things had not been "that bad." Like most people, she had heard all sorts of horror stories about living with alcoholics. Molly's own father had often drunk too much, and that had been hard on her mother and the children. But they had all survived. Until recently Hank had been a good father, if not a good husband. Oh, he fought all the time with Ryan—but he often joked and laughed with the smaller ones. They had always had enough to eat and usually enough money to take care of the demands of raising five children. Except for that recent incident with Ryan, he had never been violent. And he never had actually touched Bobbie; he had just made crude remarks.

No, none of that seemed really outrageous. They were all things that could be explained.

The things that she thought about the longest were the little things—the promises. She thought all husbands had probably promised sometime to be home for dinner by five and hadn't shown up till seven. But Hank had done it countless times. How many times, after the kids had gone to bed, had they argued about it and had he promised to cut down on his drinking and get home earlier? But he hadn't. How many times had he said they'd get away for a weekend, just the two of them? And they hadn't. How many times had they argued in the morning and she thought about the things he accused her of all day long? How often had she then searched and searched for what she was doing wrong in their relationship only to have him come home in the evening acting as if nothing had happened? Those were the things Molly thought and wrote about. Before she knew it, the room was getting light and it was time to start another day. She thought to herself that this intervention had better come soon, or she'd forget how to sleep.

But she had dragged herself through other days, sleepless and worn. Maybe she'd get a nap this afternoon.

CHAPTER XI

I<small>F</small> Molly thought she needed any help to get her through the day, Sally took care of that at the breakfast table. Hank asked why no one was home when he had tried to call last night, and everyone looked at Molly. All but Sally.

"We all went to the hospital and talked to some man," she said. When she looked around at the faces that swung quickly to look at her she said, "Oh-oh!" and covered her mouth.

"What man?" Hank asked, and this time all the looks went to Molly. She knew she had to say something, but she wasn't sure if the words were stuck in the lump in her throat or the knot in her gut.

"We went to see a counselor," Molly finally got out.

"What do you mean, 'counselor'? At what hospital? Who's sick?" The questions poured from Hank quicker than Molly could find answers. She tried to put him off.

"I'll talk to you about it tonight."

"Tonight nothing. I want to know now," Hank said, banging his fist on the table, which bounced the cereal bowls for emphasis.

"Children, you had better leave for school," Molly said, and even though they hadn't finished their breakfast, no one argued. Within seconds the house was quiet and empty except for Molly and Hank. As soon as the door closed, Hank glared at Molly.

"I'm waiting," was all he said.

"We're seeing a family counselor at the Alcoholism Treatment Center." Molly felt like she had squeezed each of those words from her insides. Hank just stared at her for a moment in disbelief. Molly could see his face turn red and was sure his blood pressure was rising. She wasn't sure which of the many thoughts that must be running through his head he would jump on first.

"You bitch," he said. "You're trying to turn my family against me!"

Molly was frightened. He was speaking through his teeth, in hushed tones she had never heard before.

"In the first place," she said, "we are going there for ourselves and not for you. We all need help—someone to talk to about what's troubling us. I think you could use help, too.

"And you don't need anyone to help in alienating your family; you've been doing a good enough job yourself lately doing that in this house."

She saw his face relax just a little, and that helped her relax also.

"Just make sure you take care of your own problems and I'll take care of mine," he said. Then—as he always did—without waiting to hear what she might have to say he got up and left. Normally when he did that it frustrated Molly, but this time she felt relieved. Rather than think about what had occurred she, too, left quickly for school.

On the way she stopped at an intersection where she normally turned left. Instead she did the first irresponsible thing she could remember doing in a long time. She turned right. In the hospital lobby, she phoned the school to tell them she'd be late and then called the hospital to get Josh's room number. She used the back stairs, since she knew visiting hours wouldn't begin for hours. Walking down the corridor, she tried to act as if she belonged there. When she was halfway down the hall to Josh's room she heard a voice calling from behind her.

"Miss!" the voice said. She knew instantly it was a nurse calling to her. She ignored it and continued toward Josh's room.

"Miss!" the voice called out again. Again she ignored the nurse and continued to walk. A smile crossed her face. This was twice in one day she was ignoring what she was supposed to do—and she hadn't broken in half. If she could just get a few more feet without the voice overtaking her, she would reach Josh and perhaps he could influence the nurse to let her stay.

By the time she reached Josh's room she could almost feel the nurse's breath on her back. She turned and pushed open the door and there he was. He looked thin and pale but also peaceful. She stood and gazed at him for just a moment, when the now irritated voice startled her.

"Miss, visiting hours are not until this afternoon." Molly turned and looked the nurse in the eye. Her voice was calm but firm.

"I work in the afternoon and have children to attend to in the evening. This man has been my best friend for years and in this hospital almost a week and this is my first opportunity to see him."

"I'm sorry, Miss, but rules are rules," the nurse said. Molly stared at her a moment.

"People are more important than rules," she said, and turned to Josh's bed. She could see his eyes were open and he seemed to be watching with amusement.

"Miss, if you don't leave I'll have to call an orderly," the nurse said.

Gosh, this lady is persistent, Molly thought.

"You'll have to do that," Molly said. "In fact, you'd better get two."

"Nurse, let her stay," a soft voice finally chipped in from the bed. A deep sigh of frustration and resignation came from the nurse.

"All right, Doctor." As she left, she turned to Molly. "I'll be back in fifteen minutes, and then you'll have to go."

When Molly turned back to Josh both of them were smiling. She stood there for a moment just drinking in the peace and serenity this frail man offered.

"You could have spoken sooner," she said with the smile still in her eyes.

"Didn't think you needed any help; looked like you could have had that nurse for breakfast," he said with the smile still covering his whole face.

The room grew silent. The two friends looked at each other and did all their talking in a few brief looks, then confirmed it with words over the remainder of the visit.

Molly spoke first.

"I'm sorry about our last visit," she said. "I still don't know if it's going to help, but we are proceeding with the intervention."

He looked at her and said, "It already has."

She looked puzzled, but thought she understood.

"Yes," she said. "But there has been pain, too. Scott hasn't been home from college or called since we've started. It's brought up unpleasant memories for all of us, and we haven't even done the intervention yet. Hank told me this morning that he thought I was turning his family against him."

"Change is difficult and painful, but I believe you are giving your family choices they didn't have before," Josh said.

"I know," said Molly. "I just hope it works."

"I hope so, too," said Josh. "I'll be praying for you. When will it take place?"

"I'm not sure. We still have two meetings before we meet with Hank."

"Molly, I wish you the best." The compassion in Josh's face and voice almost embraced Molly. She stood for a moment wrapped up in it like a blanket. His next statement shocked her out of her comfort.

"It should never have taken this long."

"What do you mean?" Molly asked defensively.

"I should have encouraged you much sooner to do this," Josh said, "but so many things got in the way. One was my own ignorance. It's only been recently that the medical profession has recognized alcoholism as a disease, and even now we don't get adequate training in it. It is so different, too, in terms of treatment. Usually we give patients drugs, not try to take them away.

"Then there was me and my own feelings. I don't think I've told you how much your friendship has meant to me. You have filled a big void in my life, and I was afraid of losing that. I knew I would have to confront and push you in order to make this happen. I was afraid it would end our friendship. I let my personal feelings and my fear of confrontation get in the way of my professional obligations.

"The only thing I regret is that perhaps I allowed our friendship to stop me from pushing you harder to get help and that may have hurt you and your family."

"Time's up."

The nurse stood at the door with an orderly on each side of her. Molly was at a loss. She bent down and gave Josh a quick kiss on his cheek.

"See you soon," she said. She left quickly, without looking back.

Molly drove back to school in numb disbelief. She was angry at Josh for misjudging the depth of their friendship. She could think of nothing he could have said or done to her that could have destroyed the bond between them. Why was he so insecure about it?

Yet she also felt sorry that she hadn't told him that. She turned on the radio and sang with the music to drown out her feelings.

CHAPTER XII

Whenever Ken was working close to home, he stopped for lunch. Today he drove up slowly and stuck his head in the door gingerly. Martha had spoke very little to him since the night they had gone to the first intervention meeting. She was sitting on the couch, reading. "Anything for lunch?" he asked.

"Nothing much. I haven't been to the store," she commented, not looking up from her book. Ken sat beside her. She continued to read.

"What are you reading?" he asked.

"A book," she replied.

"Don't you think this has gone on long enough?" he challenged. She finally looked up from her book, but said nothing.

"You know what I mean," he persisted. "You haven't said ten words to me since we came home the other night."

"I think you're making a mistake," she said, "but I can't convince you of that. So why should I talk?"

"Any time poor Martha doesn't get her way she pouts," he said with obvious sarcasm.

Now Martha threw her book down and glared at Ken. "My way? My way?" she stormed. "Through this whole thing all I've ever said is, 'Ken, what about your business?' 'Ken, he's your brother.' 'What if it doesn't work?' 'He may never speak to you again.' I've only been concerned about you through this whole thing, and now you say I've got to have my way. That really hurts, Ken." Then she started to cry.

Ken showed no interest in her tears. "You know," he said, "I've always been afraid that because I give in to you so often you'd think I wasn't a man, but I loved you and didn't want to lose you, so I took that chance. But it surprises me that you think I'm stupid. Don't you think I can see through this phony concern for me?"

The tears stopped. The expression on Martha's face showed rage, then amazement, then slowly softened before she spoke. "O.K., Ken. The truth is, I don't like your brother, and I never have. Even though you have achieved a lot more than he, he still wants to treat you as his kid brother. I'm afraid if this intervention works you'll want to start spending time with Hank and Molly again, and that seems like drudgery to me."

Ken's voice also softened. "I'm sorry you don't like Hank, but he's my brother and I care about him, so I'm going through with this. But I'll understand if you don't want to be a part of it."

"You know," she said, "it seems funny to hear you say you're afraid of losing me, because I'm terrified of losing you. I don't want your brother to take you from me. I don't have any friends. You're all I have and when you're gone— no matter what I'm doing—I'm thinking of you coming home. You're right: I am selfish. I don't want to share you. I think it would be better if I didn't go to the intervention.

"But I promise I'll give your brother another chance if he gets sober."

Ken took Martha's hand and smiled at her.

"Sorry there's nothing for lunch," she said, smiling and stroking his face, "but it doesn't have to be a wasted trip."

His voice was husky as he said, "It hasn't been." Then he picked her up and carried her, giggling, to the bedroom.

CHAPTER XIII

THE group—minus two original members, Bobbie and Martha—gathered again in Jack's office the next Monday night. Jack set up two films for them to watch. The first was called "The Enablers." It was about a woman alcoholic and her family, but Molly had no trouble identifying with it. She thought to herself how much families must have in common where alcohol plays such a big role. She could even see how some of the patterns in her parents' marriage were repeating themselves in hers. She decided right there that, whatever happened in the intervention, she would join an Al-Anon group she had heard of and she would encourage the kids to go to Al-Anon or Al-Ateen.

The second film was called "The Intervention." It showed explicitly how to set up an intervention. When Molly saw the alcoholic walk into the room with all the people waiting, she thought the knot in her stomach would never again come unraveled. She wondered if she could ever go through with this, and if she did, what Hank would do to them for putting him through it. But the movie ended on a positive note. The alcoholic agreed to go into treatment. Once again, Molly had a flicker of hope.

After the films were over they gathered in the room with Jack. He asked them first how many had written down what they wanted to say. Molly was surprised that she was the only one who had. Jack didn't seem angry or surprised. He simply said, "As you can probably tell from the movie, when the time comes to confront Hank there's going to be a lot of tension. If you have your statement written out, you'll feel more comfortable. You can refer to it or just read it aloud." He looked at each of them in turn, speaking very carefully.

"We may only have one chance at this, and I don't think you want to lose it because someone is too nervous to say his or her part."

"You don't have to worry about me," Ryan said. "I've been waiting all my life for a time when I can talk and my dad has to listen." Jack smiled, as did everyone else.

"O.K.," Jack said. "We have several things to do tonight. I want to hear what each of you has to say, and give you some ideas about how to say it with more impact. But most of all I want to teach you to say it in a way that won't make Hank defensive. Then we have to decide who will go first, second, and so on. We have to decide on the day and the time of the intervention and how you will all get here. I want the rest of you here at least fifteen minutes before Molly and Hank. The night before the intervention we'll practice one more time. Molly, since you are the only one who wrote anything, let's hear you first."

Molly was startled. She felt embarrassed to read what she had written in front of the others. She was no stranger to writing; she often had written things in a journal she kept in the "circular file." She'd write her thoughts and feelings down on paper, then burn it or tear it up and throw it away. It sometimes was the only thing that kept her sane. But to read out loud what she wrote—that was another matter.

"I don't think I should be first in the intervention," she said, directing her eyes at Jack.

"I agree," said Jack. "By this time Hank is immune to what you say. But for now, go first."

Molly started slowly. "Hank," she said. "Do you remember when we were first married and we would sit and talk for hours?"

"I hate to interrupt already," Jack said, "but don't start out with a question to Hank. Remember, we want him to listen, not talk. So don't give him the opportunity to take the floor. Start out with, 'I remember. . . .' "

Molly started over. "I remember when. . . ." and continued with the many times he had promised to quit and hadn't—how it hurt her to see his sharp mind disappear in the fog of drinking and hangovers. When she had finished, Jack spoke again.

"That was very good, but you need to include more specifics and more about how you feel. Here's a general outline you can use: start with 'Hank, I love you,' then a description of his behavior. But when you describe it, avoid words that are judgmental like, 'You were drunk.' Just say 'You were drinking' or 'You had had several drinks.' Then describe how you felt. End by saying 'I love you' or 'I care about you and I want you to get help!' "

Ryan was the next to share.

"Dad," he started, "a few weeks ago I came home after I had been drinking. You were asleep on the couch and I went into the bathroom and I was throwing up. Mom and Bobbie came into the bathroom to help and we woke you up from your nap. . . ." He related the whole incident, spitting the words out one by one. At the end he spoke of being angry and disgusted. He said he was frightened the next morning of what his father might say but wasn't surprised that Hank didn't remember what had happened.

"That's excellent data," Jack said, "but can you think of how else you felt besides angry and disgusted? You see, if your dad is like other people I've worked with—and I suspect he is— he'll be looking for a way to get the heat off of him. The best way to do that is to get into an argument with someone who's angry at him and who's had a lot of practice arguing with him before. I suspect that's you on both counts."

"But I am angry with him," Ryan protested.

"I know that," Jack said, "and it sounds as though you have a right to be, but what else did you feel when that event occurred?"

"Just anger," Ryan replied.

"Think about it," Jack said gently. "If it had happened to me I think I would have felt a lot of other things, too, but I don't want to speak for you."

Paul spoke next.

"Dad, I love you," he said. "I remember a time when I was small. Ryan had some friends

over and they were playing baseball in the back-
yard. I wanted to play, too, but they said I was
too young and I wasn't good enough. I was
crying when you came home and you asked me
what was wrong. You came close and I could
smell liquor on your breath and when you picked
me up we both almost fell over. I told you
about what Ryan and his friends had said. You
went up to Ryan and made him give you the
ball. You kept throwing it to him so hard his
hand was hurting and if he missed it you mocked
him and said he wasn't good enough to play
with you. All his friends went home. I was
embarrassed for Ryan and afraid that he would
think I had put you up to it.

"I remember another time that Scott had a
girl over to the house in the evening. She was
real nice and they were letting me stay in the
room and talk to them. You had been drinking
all day and were in the bedroom, but you came
out to get a beer from the refrigerator. You
had only your underwear on, but you walked
right in front of them and even stopped to talk.
You slurred your words so it was hard to understand what you were saying. You told me to
get out of there because they wanted to neck.
I left, but I could see that both Scott and the
girl were real embarrassed. I never saw that girl
again.

"I began to think it was better not to have friends than to be embarrassed like that."

"I love you, Dad, but please get help." Paul's voice shook on the last few words.

Everyone in the silent room stared at Paul.

"That's perfect," Jack said. Molly thought she heard amazement even in his voice. Paul smiled broadly in a way Molly had never seen before this moment. She asked herself when the last time was that Paul had been complimented, and she couldn't remember.

"I'm sorry about the pain you've been carrying around, Paul," Molly told him, "but it certainly is beautiful the way you've expressed it. If I was your father, I certainly would go for help." Paul smiled all the wider.

"That brings up another important point," Jack said. "What happens if in spite of your best efforts here, Hank doesn't go for treatment?"

Molly's heart sank, and she suddenly realized how much she was beginning to believe this would work. Now her old doubts came crashing back. It doesn't take much to cut through hope—it's such a slender thread, she thought.

Ken spoke up first.

"Well, as I said before, Hank is an excellent worker, so I can't threaten to fire him. Our personal relationship has deteriorated anyway. So I guess for me not much will have changed."

"I'll have to think about it," Molly said.

"You wouldn't leave Daddy, would you, Mommy?" Sally asked in a frightened voice.

"No, Honey, I don't think I would," Molly said carefully. "But we can't continue as we have been, either. I'll have to think about it."

A pained look came over Sally's face.

"Would you like to do yours next?" Jack asked Sally. The little girl still looked sad, but it gave way to a slight smile and a look of importance. "I'm not ready with mine yet," she said. "I'll think about it and tell you next time." Molly smiled. Jack looked as though he was about to push her to come up with something, when Molly waved him off.

"That's O.K.," she said. "You can wait, Sally. But make sure you're ready next time. What you say to Daddy is very important."

Finally Ken gave his speech. His nieces and nephews were amazed by the way he talked about their father. Thank God for Ken, Molly thought. Hank will listen to him if he'll listen to anybody.

"O.K.," Jack said when Ken finished, "that's it for tonight. What we have to do next is schedule a time when we can get Hank in here. Then we'll meet the night before to decide on the order and to practice the intervention." They all got up to leave, except Molly.

She was lost in thought. How would she ever get Hank to come willingly to his own intervention?

CHAPTER XIV

MOLLY wondered all the way home how she was going to get Hank to agree to go to counseling, especially because things had been better at home since she had raised the subject. He was coming home at night in time for dinner, staying awake after dinner and even helping the children with their homework. He talked and laughed with them the way he used to do.

A few days passed without her having the courage to ask him. Then the opportunity presented itself. It was the first really warm day of spring. Molly loved to open the windows and let the spring air rush through the house, blowing out all the air that seemed to have been trapped inside all winter long.

Hank was late for dinner, so Molly fed the children and kept Hank's dinner in the oven as she often did. As they were finishing dinner they heard the car pull into the driveway and then a crash. At the noise, Ryan's face went pale. Molly turned to him immediately.

"What's the matter?" she asked, with dread in her voice.

"I left my bike in the driveway," Ryan said. The whole family knew what that meant. Hank had a "thing" about stuff in the driveway. Even when he was sober it upset him, but when he was drinking it became the moral equivalent of an assassination attempt.

"Ryan! Get out here," he shouted.

"Mommy, I'm scared. Will Daddy hurt Ryan?" Sally asked. Molly thought for a second.

"Ryan get out here," Hank yelled again. Molly thought it was fortunate that Hank's concern about the driveway even included her car. She always parked it on the street before he was home, because he told her she didn't know how to pull it into the garage. So she always let him pull in first, then drove hers in later.

"Bobbie," she spoke in a hushed voice so Hank would not hear her through the open windows. "Take my car and take the children to Uncle Ken's house. Go out the front door when Dad comes in the back. Don't come back home till I call you."

"Ryan! I know you're in there," Hank shouted again.

The kids stood by the front door until they heard their father come in the back. Then they silently left.

Hank had some trouble negotiating the steps and the door into the house, which gave them some extra time. Molly sat quietly at the table.

"Where is he?" he asked.

"Who?" she asked.

"You know perfectly well who," Hank said. "And where is everyone else?"

"I sent them away," Molly answered.

He looked at her sternly. "I'm tired of dragging things out of you, Molly. What the hell is going on?"

"I sent them away because they're afraid of you when you're like this. And frankly, Hank, so am I," Molly said. She was surprised at the calmness in her voice. She knew that later, when the impact of what she was doing finally hit her, she'd be shaking for hours.

"Well then, they just left," Hank roared. "I'll just go find them."

"If you get in that car I will go right to the phone and call the police. I'll tell them you're drunk and the direction you're heading," Molly said firmly, but still calmly. She could feel herself shaking inside.

"Why are you doing this to me, Molly? Why are you trying to take my children from me?" Hank asked in a pleading voice that surprised Molly. She realized that he was genuinely confused. Confused by his own denial. She felt some compassion for him.

"I don't want to take your children from you, Hank, but when you're drinking like this and you get so angry, I'm afraid you'll hurt them," she said.

"Oh bullshit!" he said. "That's just all the nonsense you're probably getting from that counseling crap."

"Why don't you come with me and make sure that they don't brainwash me?" Molly said in as inviting a manner as she could. She was proud of herself for thinking so quickly. Usually she'd think of an idea that good later, and wish she'd said it.

"I'll just have to do that," he said. Then he went back out to the driveway to try to remove Ryan's bike from under the car.

Molly knew that it was Hank's bravado and booze talking. Still, he had agreed and she thought it was enough of a commitment that she could use it on him later. He stayed outside quite a while. Every once in a while she could hear him curse some more. He gradually got quieter, though, and after a while she heard only mumbles. She decided to go out to him.

"Need any help?" she asked.

"Damn handlebar is caught in the bumper," he muttered.

Together they worked and finally got the bike loose. Afterward, they went inside and had supper. Hank was quiet during the meal, and Molly sat and bided her time. She wasn't sure how much he had had to drink. She had no way of telling for sure if he would remember the conversation in the morning. He seemed calmer, but she knew that the wrong words might just set him off again.

Finally he broke the silence. "Why aren't those kids back yet? Where did you send them— to China?" She wasn't sure what to say.

She finally decided to risk the truth. "I told them to go to see your brother. I told them I'd call them when they should come home."

Molly got up and went to the phone. She called Ken and told him to send the children home. She whispered into the phone, "He's agreed to come. Tell Ryan to apologize to him as soon as he gets home."

CHAPTER XV

THE next day, Molly called Jack and set up a time for the intervention: eight o'clock on the following Tuesday morning. They agreed to meet the evening before to practice.

In the evening, when Hank came home, she gave him time to have dinner and take a nap. Shortly after he awoke, she sat next to him on the couch.

"We're set to go to the counselor at eight on Tuesday morning," she said. She could tell by the look of pain and disgust on his face that it was not going to be easy to convince him to go.

"I can't go then. I work during the day, you know."

"Ken will let you off if you tell him you have a doctor's appointment," she said calmly.

"He's my brother. I'm not going to lie to him—and besides, we're running way behind on the deadline for those new apartments. I can't leave him short-handed like that."

"Then tell him the truth. Or tell him you're going to the hospital for a check-up. That isn't a lie," Molly responded. "I know Ken depends on you heavily, but certainly he can get along without you for a few hours." She saw him shaking his head, and knew she had not convinced him.

"Would you like me to call for you and ask your boss for permission?" Molly asked. She tried not to say it sarcastically, and hoped she had succeeded. But she knew that his pride would not allow this to continue.

"I don't need anyone to do my asking for me," he said. "I can get off if I want to, but I don't like to take advantage of my brother that way."

"You are the best, most consistent worker he's got. You never even take a sick day, even when you're sick." She wanted to say "no matter how hung over you are," but thought better of it. She was trying to appeal to his pride, not start another fight. Besides, she really was amazed at the discipline it must have taken for him to drag himself from bed on those "mornings after." People who thought that people who had trouble with alcohol were just weak-willed had never seen Hank pull himself out of bed after a night of heavy drinking.

"This is really important to me, Hank. Please call him and ask him." She picked up the phone and handed it towards him.

"I'll ask him tomorrow at work," he said.

"No," she said, "you'll get busy and forget."

He grabbed the phone.

"Oh, all right. God! you've become a nag."

He called Ken. Molly knew right away that Martha must have answered the phone by the coolness in his voice. Without identifying himself, Hank asked to speak to Ken.

"Ken," he started, "would you please tell my wife that we are too busy right now for her to be scheduling appointments for me at the hospital during working hours?" He was smiling now and was getting ready to hand her the phone when his expression changed. Molly knew that Ken had caught on.

"But you know how busy we are," Hank said. He was unable to hide his surprise and disappointment that his brother was unwilling to go along with his obvious lead.

"It's Tuesday," he said. "I'll only be away a few hours, I guess." There was a lost puppy tone to his voice. He handed Molly the phone.

"O.K.," he said, "but I hope you're not expecting too much out of this."

A quiet "Thanks, Ken," was all Molly could manage before she hung up.

Now, she thought, if I can just keep this ship afloat through the weekend.

CHAPTER XVI

THE weekend proved uneventful. Neither Hank nor any of his children mentioned the intervention, and Hank did not drink at all. Even Sunday services were uneventful, although the congregation did seem to try to sing a little more than usual.

The calm before the storm, Molly thought.

The remaining group gathered in Jack's office the night before the intervention to practice.

"This is our last chance to get our act together before the morning," Jack said. "We have to decide what order you're going to go in. And this time, I'm going to play Hank's role and respond the way he might tomorrow, to make it all the more realistic."

"Now, who should go first? It should be someone who has some influence with him."

"Well, that is surely not me," Molly said.

"I suppose I should go," Ryan said with a laugh.

"How about you, Ken?" Molly asked.

"It's probably good to start with someone who's not an immediate family member," Jack commented. "That is likely to have a calming influence."

"Well, if you think it's best," Ken said. "But remember, I'm Hank's younger brother, so don't expect miracles."

"But he respects you and you're his boss," Molly said.

"I know that," Ken said, "but I have to tell him right off that I'm not here as his boss, just as his brother and friend."

"That may make him feel less threatened and more willing to listen," said Jack.

"Well, if that's what you think best, I'll do it," Ken said, "but I don't think I'll sleep too well tonight."

"I think it might also be good if you sit next to him, Ken," Jack said. "I want each person to know where they're going to be sitting tomorrow and we'll only leave one chair open for Hank. I want him to sit by people who can be supportive, but also who can calm him down if he gets upset."

"Boy! you don't leave much to chance, do you Mr. Peterson?" Ryan said.

"Not if I can help it," Jack answered. "There will be enough tension here tomorrow to cut it and serve it up in large slices," he said, "so the more each person is prepared, the bigger advantage we have that it will come off smoothly ... and that it will have more of an effect on Hank than on us."

"You make it sound as though Dad's our enemy," Paul said.

Jack turned to look at Paul for a moment, then around the room at the rest of the family.

"Based on the data you've given me, I have no doubt that Hank has a life-threatening disease that many people deny right up to the moment when it kills them," Jack said seriously. "No, Hank is not your enemy; the disease and his denial are. We have to get through his denial, or you will all suffer, including him."

Jack was intense as he spoke. Molly hoped that he had made an impact on the children. It seemed so, because they quickly decided who would sit where. They also agreed on the order in which the rest of them would speak—Ryan, Molly, Sally, then Paul.

"I think we're ready to start after two more things are decided," Jack said. "Molly, you and Hank should come together, alone. Ken, can you pick up the children at school or at their bus stops and bring them here?"

"Sure," Ken replied.

"Good," said Jack. "I'd like you to be here at least 15 minutes before the eight o'clock starting time.

"Second, if Hank agrees to get help you must decide on what treatment you want to insist upon. I think he should go through treatment before attending A.A., but he doesn't have to pick this facility. There is one in the next town over. He can also choose between inpatient and outpatient treatment."

Molly spoke up quickly. "I agree that Hank needs treatment, if not for himself then for me. I don't think I would believe he was not drinking if he just attended A.A. meetings. Besides I think we all need the help that a treatment center can provide. I've learned to feel comfortable here, so let's offer him treatment as an outpatient here."

Everyone quickly agreed, for by now they were all following Molly's leadership. It was a new experience for all of them.

"Now," Jack said, "let's pretend that I'm Hank and that I have just walked in with Molly.

He may make a comment or two, but he'll probably be too surprised to say much. After he sits down I (as Jack) will say to him 'Hello, Hank. I'm glad you could come. These people are here today because they have some things they'd like to share with you. Are you willing to listen?' He will probably agree. At that, I will turn it over to you and it's pretty much your show. I will talk only if Hank gets defensive and argumentative. If so, I'll say, 'Hank, you promised you'd listen.'

"Now I'll put on my other hat and become Hank. Call me 'Hank' or 'Dad' when you talk to me. It will help you to get more completely into what is going to happen tomorrow."

They started the intervention, speaking in the order on which they had agreed. Ken went first, and stuck closely to the script he had followed in the earlier practice session. Jack, role playing Hank, made a few comments but mostly just listened. Ken finished with, "I love you and I want you to get help."

"Dad," Ryan said next, "a few weeks ago I came home after drinking. I threw up in the bathroom and Mom and Bobbie were taking care of me, but you had to come in and you seemed worse off than me. You were yelling at me for being drunk and I said 'It takes one to know one,' and you just stuck my head in the toilet. If Mom hadn't stopped you, you might have drowned me. I felt so angry at you that I wanted to forget you were my father. The next morning you acted like you didn't even remember."

Molly turned to Jack. She knew that he would start an argument with Ryan and hoped Ryan would see through it. Sure enough Jack, role playing Hank, jumped on Ryan's comment.

"Well, what are you doing coming home drunk?" he said.

"Imitating you, what do you think?" Ryan answered sharply.

"You think you have permission to act like a smart ass because you have all these people around?" Jack shot back.

"Yes. For a change you're the one who has to take some heat in this family instead of me," Ryan said.

"Maybe that's because no one screws up as much as you do," Jack said.

"Mommy, he sounds just like Daddy at the kitchen table," Sally said.

Jack waved his arms. "Wait a minute. I have to speak for a moment as myself. Ryan, remember you can't argue with him. If he hooks you in that way, he takes the attention off himself.

You're going to have to control your anger or it would be better for you not to be here. Try starting with some other feelings besides anger. What else did you feel besides anger?"

Ryan put his head down and shook his head. "I don't know. When I think of him I only see red. Besides, even if I could think of other feelings I don't think I trust him enough to give him the satisfaction of knowing. I just don't think I can do this. I'm sorry Mom."

Molly's heart sank. She looked at Jack.

"Can we do this with only four people?"

"I'd like to have more," he said, "but we've come too far to turn back now. We'll do the best we can. Ryan, you can still help out. I'd like you to role play your father for the rest of the intervention."

"I'll try, but I don't know if I can act like him," Ryan said.

"Why not?" said Jack quickly. "You act just like him. He's angry all the time and so are you."

CHAPTER XVII

For Bobbie, the day started out as usual. She dressed herself and then helped Sally get dressed. "Now you have to be a big brave girl today, O.K.?" she told her little sister in a soft voice.

"I will, Bobbie," said Sally, "but it would be easier if you would be there."

"Shhhh!" Bobbie put her finger to her mouth. "Daddy doesn't know you'll be there, so we have to keep it a secret till he arrives."

Tears filled Sally's eyes. "What if I make a mistake?" she asked.

"Just do what you can, Honey," Bobbie answered. "No one can ask more of you than that." Bobbie gave her sister a hug and held her for a long time. When she finally let go, Sally seemed to be better. Bobbie put her arm around Sally and they walked down together to breakfast.

Molly was already cooking breakfast. She felt tired, but she was sure the events of the day would quickly cause her to rally. Paul and Ryan soon joined them in the kitchen. They were all sitting at the breakfast table when Hank joined them. They all looked up quietly as he entered the room.

"Good morning," he said to them. They all sat quietly. "What's the matter with you kids? You act like you've seen a ghost." His voice sounded irritated. Molly thought quickly.

"They're not used to seeing you at this time. You're usually gone to work before they're even up."

"Yeah, Dad, you playing hooky today?" Ryan asked with a smile. Hank looked back at him like he didn't appreciate Ryan's humor, so Ryan looked down to continue his breakfast.

The children ate quickly and left, and Molly breathed a sigh as they left. She looked at the clock. It was seven fifteen. She wondered if she could last the next half hour. She went up and showered for as long as she could, then dressed slowly. She came down and cleaned up the kitchen and still had five minutes to kill before leaving. Hank was still sitting at the kitchen table drinking coffee. He was dressed, but hadn't shaved.

"Don't you think you should shave before we go?" she asked meekly.

"I plan to," Hank said.

"We really should be leaving pretty quick."

"One morning I don't have to go to work and can linger over a cup of coffee, and you've got to rush me." His voice sounded angry. Molly knew he would like nothing better than to get into a fight and then storm out so he could get out of going.

"I'm sorry," she said, "take your time."

He did that. He sipped slowly on his coffee then took forever shaving, but Molly kept quiet. When they finally left it was almost eight. Luckily the hospital was not far away. Molly knew it would be a quiet car ride. On the way over she busied herself worrying about the children. She wondered if Ken had picked them up, and how they were feeling. She even wondered about how Ryan and Bobbie would feel not being there.

Ken had picked up the two youngest children at their bus stop by seven thirty and was at the hospital by twenty to eight. They all came into the room and sat in their assigned places. The room was as quiet as Molly's car as their eyes roamed from the clock to the door and back to the clock.

When Molly and Hank finally arrived, Molly walked into the room first and sat in her seat, leaving only one remaining chair for Hank. He looked angry and confused. Jack stood up and shook his hand.

"Hank, I'm glad you could come. My name is Jack Peterson and I believe you know the rest of these people. They are here today because they care about you and they have some things they'd like to tell you. Are you willing to listen?"

Hank looked around the room. No one looked at him but Jack.

"I don't like surprises," Hank said.

"I can understand that," Jack said, "but will you listen?"

"Yeah, I'll listen," was Hank's gruff reply.

CHAPTER XVIII

A<small>T</small> the high school, Bobbie was unusually fidgety in her homeroom. She glared at Tom, who sat next to her. She had been in school with him since grade school and they were exact opposites. She never got in trouble and he was rarely out of it. Their classmates often teased them about liking one another, but Bobbie acted as if she hated him. The homeroom teacher was out of the room, so of course he was acting up.

While she was watching him, he stopped abruptly. When she looked to the front of the room it was not difficult to figure out why. The dean had walked in, and he was a six-foot-two ex-marine who looked as if he could have Tom for lunch. But he called Bobbie to the front of the room and spoke to her softly.

"The homeroom teacher is ill and we're having trouble finding a substitute. Would you look after the class please?" He really didn't bother to wait for an answer. "Just write the names of those who cause trouble on a list and they'll get a detention. Take roll and bring any absences to my office on your way to the next class." The dean never questioned that she'd do it, or considered how she'd feel turning in a list of her classmates for detention. This was the reputation Bobbie had at the small high school. She was considered more a peer of her teachers than of her fellow students.

Bobbie looked slightly irritated after the dean left the room, and Tom's immediate talking and laughing didn't seem to help. She tried to busy herself with the roll call, but Tom seemed unwilling to be denied her attention.

"Tom, I'm going to have to put your name on a list for detention," she said. She seemed patient enough, but Tom quickly tested it.

"Go ahead, you snitch," he responded.

"Please, Tom. I have to get the roll done," she said, trying to reason with him.

"Please, Tom. I have to get the roll done," he mocked. The camel's back had been broken.

"Why don't you grow up?" she said in a belittling manner.

"Why don't you grow down?" he said, matching her tone. She sat motionless for a moment, then tears filled her eyes. She closed the book she was working on and slowly walked from the room, carrying the book with her.

Tom didn't seem frightened for himself when he went after her. He seemed genuinely concerned for her. His voice sounded tender when he reached her and gently grabbed her arm.

"I'm sorry, Bobbie," he said. "I guess I don't know when to quit." She didn't pull her arm from his. Instead she turned toward him and touched his face with her hand. With tears still in her eyes she looked right into his.

"You may have done me a favor," she said. Then a smile covered her face. She took a couple of steps away and threw him the roll book.

"Here, you take roll." Then she laughed at the surprised look on his face.

"Where are you going?" he asked, sounding like any parent.

"I've got some errands to run. I think I'll take the day off."

"You want company?" Tom asked with a grin.

"I've got to do these myself," she said. "We'll have to play hookey together some other day."

"I'll count on it," he said. "Don't get in trouble now," his voice sounded with a sarcastic warning.

"I think it's about time I did." Bobbie called back from down the hall. "It might just take some of the pressure off you around here."

With that they waved and Tom went back to class. Bobbie, on the other hand, went to the dean's office, not really looking for the dean as much as for Ryan. Sure enough, he was there, spending the last day of an in-school suspension.

"Ryan, we need to go to that intervention," she said.

"I've been sitting here thinking the same thing, but how?" he asked.

Ryan was sitting in the dean's outer office. The dean had his door closed. Bobbie knocked on the door.

"Don't bother. He walked out a few minutes ago," Ryan said.

Bobbie then opened the door and found the dean's sport coat hanging on the coat tree. She reached in his pocket and found his car keys.

"Let's go," she said. Ryan looked as if he'd witnessed a miracle.

"We can explain later," Bobbie said. "There's no time now."

They walked back out into the hall. Ryan would not have gotten twenty feet without being stopped by a hall monitor, but with Bobbie next to him they got to the door by the teacher's parking lot before anyone stopped them. "Where are you going?" the monitor asked. Ryan looked nervous but Bobbie quickly answered.

"We have a family emergency. The dean said we could use his car." With that, she turned and walked out and Ryan followed.

They knew which car was the dean's. All the students looked at it and drooled. It was a red sports car. When they got in and Bobbie started it and backed out, Ryan spoke with a new sense of respect.

"You've wasted your life," he said with admiration. "Crime needs people like you."

Bobbie drove quickly but safely to the treatment center.

CHAPTER XIX

A<small>T</small> the treatment center Paul had finished speaking. It had gone smoothly. Molly could tell that Hank had been moved, but not convinced. When Paul had said ". . . and I'd like you to get help," Hank had said, "Well that depends. What kind of help are we talking about?"

"We want you to go to an outpatient treatment program here," Molly said. "You could keep on working and come here for treatment in the evening and then go to A.A. meetings on the weekend."

"Why can't I just quit drinking if that's the problem?" Hank asked belligerently.

"Perhaps I can help with that one," Jack said. "First of all, most people need help and support to quit. Molly has talked about numerous times you have said you'd quit or cut down and you haven't. I believe that's because you can't quit without help. More importantly, your drinking has affected you and your family not only physically, but also emotionally and spiritually. If you only quit drinking it just takes care of the physical problems. You all need help in those other areas of your lives."

"I don't know," said Hank. "Why aren't the rest of the family here?"

Molly had given a lot of thought to that question before he ever asked it. It was one she had anticipated. She knew very well that he would think, because of his denial, that the other children didn't think he had a problem. In spite of her fear about the conclusions he would draw, she decided that she didn't want to further the lack of direct communication in the family by speaking for Scott, Bobbie and Ryan. She had interpreted his behavior to them and theirs to him long enough.

"You'll have to ask them yourself," she said.

Molly thought about how she needed to tell Hank about what would happen if he didn't stop drinking. Molly still wasn't sure what to say. She didn't want a divorce, but she was just beginning to see how the whole family was being affected by Hank's drinking and she couldn't continue to subject the children to that. She would start with the things she knew she would do and hope that Hank didn't see them as a threat.

At that moment, Bobbie and Ryan walked into the room. In that instant, Molly remembered the moments they were each born. Those wonderful moments when she counted all their arms, legs, fingers, and toes and found them all there. They were alive and healthy and the labor was over and soon forgotten. She thought this moment, seeing them enter the room, was equally blessed.

"Now, Hank," she said with tears of joy in her eyes, "you can ask them yourself."

Even though Jack had made it clear that anyone who had not participated in the final role-playing should not come to the intervention, he silently widened the circle. Bobbie and Ryan pulled up two extra chairs directly across from Hank.

"Why weren't you here for the rest of this?" Hank asked bluntly.

Ryan spoke first. His voice was different now. It was quiet and soft. He ignored his father's question and began with his own data.

"Dad, I remember a time recently when I had come home after drinking. I was throwing up in the bathroom and Bobbie and Mom were taking care of me. You came in after the noise woke you up from sleeping. You had been at the bar most of the afternoon and had missed dinner, so I guess you had drank a lot. When you saw I was sick and staggering you accused me of being drunk. I said 'It takes one to know one.' You took my head and pushed it in the toilet. I couldn't breathe and I was scared.

"Mom made you let me up, and when I came up with my face filled with vomit I felt humiliated. Mom told you we'd talk about it in the morning, but the next day you didn't remember. I was relieved, but I was angry too, like a page had been torn out of my life that would never be finished."

Hank was quiet for a moment while he tried to make sense of what he heard.

"Yes and it's stunts like that that get you in trouble all the time," Hank finally said. "Maybe we should be here talking about your drinking problem."

Ryan had a tear in his eye and his mouth went tight. Bobbie reached over and put her hand on his shoulder.

"Maybe you're right, Dad, but we're here to talk about you now," Ryan said. His voice was still soft. Molly was proud of how he controlled himself. In the past he had always been hooked into fighting with Hank, but this time he hadn't.

"What, no smart ass comment?" Hank asked.

"No, Dad, I love you and I want you to get help." Ryan said. Hank stared off in silence.

"Dad," Bobbie said. She was already crying, and had to stop until the lump left her throat.

"I'm here because I love you, but also because I love all of us. I didn't want to come here today because it was too hard for me to watch you go through this. You've always been my Dad, and even when you were drinking and making comments to me that embarrassed me, I loved you and respected you.

"But Daddy, I'm learning that we're all being hurt by your drinking. All my life I've been taking care of other people. You were drinking and Mom was concerned with your drinking and that often left me to care for the smaller kids. No one told me I had to, but I did it just to keep peace. But Daddy, I'm missing growing up. I've spent my life already being a grownup. I want to be young and have fun like other kids. I want Paul to have friends and Ryan to show his good side. I want Scott to be human instead of perfect and I want Sally to be less confused.

"Please, Daddy, get help so we can all get better."

At the start of the intervention Hank had reminded Molly of the Wisconsin winters. He had been cold and frozen. When his brother talked he became like a mild day in January. He was pleasant enough but there was no hint of a thaw. Through each person's talk she saw a warming trend but still could only hope for springtime. When Ryan spoke so softly she knew spring was coming and with Bobbie it was confirmed when the ice in Hank melted and ran down his checks.

When he nodded his head "yes" he was sobbing like the stores of past frozen winters had broken loose. When the family gathered around him and touched him, it truly felt like summer.

"What do you want me to do?" he asked his family when he had stopped crying.

"We would like you to go now and get admitted into the outpatient program," Ken told him. "You could be finished by noon and even come to work if you wanted. Though you're more than welcome to the day off."

"With or without pay?" Hank quipped lamely.

Ken smiled. "With," he said, "but you'll have to take a vacation day."

Then for the first time either could remember, the two brothers hugged.

Jack took Hank to be admitted. The family stood in a circle, holding hands. Molly looked up to heaven. "Thank God," she said simply. It was more than an expression.

Ken took Sally and Paul back to their school. Waiting for Hank, Molly sat smiling at Ryan and Bobbie. When she was about to thank them, they blurted out together, "Mom, we have a confession to make."

They told her the whole story. She tried for a while to look stern, but she was just too happy and relieved. Besides, she kind of liked the idea of Bobbie breaking a few rules for a change.

Molly called the dean, who was understandably upset but also relieved to find his car was safe. Bobbie got her first detention ever, but the dean agreed not to press charges against them. The idea of the detention didn't bother Bobbie much, since she knew Tom would undoubtedly be there with her. She thought it was time that she checked out the rumors that had floated around since grade school about the two of them.

CHAPTER XX

MOLLY spent the rest of the morning with Hank, getting him set in the outpatient treatment program. After they were finished, they took themselves out to lunch. They talked about the program they would be going through as a family. Hank admitted being scared and still somewhat in shock. He said he wanted to return to work and do something familiar for a while.

Molly's first thought was, "What happens after work?" But she didn't want to mention it and was glad when Hank said it would seem strange not stopping afterwards for a beer.

"I guess I'll be home early," he joked.

Molly decided to take the rest of the day off and go to see Josh at the hospital and tell him the good news. She slipped up the same back stairway, then down the same corridor. As she turned the corner she saw the same nurse standing in front of his room. She thought to herself that after what she had been through this lady was no match for her. Approaching the nurse, Molly thought that the woman didn't even look as mean as she did before. As a matter of fact, she looked almost sad. What was happening hit Molly as she walked even closer and saw the tears in the nurse's eyes. Molly began to shake her head and run toward the room, trying to bypass the nurse. But the nurse grabbed her around the waist.

"There's no one in there," the nurse said. "He died this morning."

Molly stopped struggling and the nurse turned her gently and held her.

"No," Molly cried. "God wouldn't do this to us. We deserve this one day to share together. Josh made this day for me. He has the right to know about it. After all the work and planning and tension I deserve one day just to enjoy it."

"I'm sorry," the nurse said. "He died peacefully this morning. There was no sign of pain or struggle."

Josh had told them less than a month ago that he was dying. Perhaps others were prepared for this, but to Molly it was a complete shock. She had been so busy with the intervention that she had no time for grieving. The last time she saw the doctor he had looked very ill, but he had been alert and talkative.

The memory of the last visit suddenly came flooding back to her. How she had been hurried out of the room after he had talked about his fear of losing her friendship. How she had never been able to respond. She pushed herself away from the nurse.

"How important do your damn visiting hours seem to you now?" Molly yelled. "The last time I saw him you had to make sure I wasn't there more than 15 minutes."

"I'm sorry," the nurse replied gently.

"You're full of those today, after it's too late, aren't you?" Molly said with fury in her voice. Then she was instantly sorry for her outrage.

"I guess I'm the one who should apologize," Molly said to the nurse. "I just can't believe he's gone." She began to cry. She cried for the loss of their relationship and the things she never had a chance to say; for the things she didn't know she felt and the thoughts she still had to sort out in her mind.

Suddenly, Molly felt exhausted. This was just too much for one day. She left the hospital and drove home slowly, just barely able to keep her eyes open enough to see the road. When she arrived at home she went to the couch and fell asleep. She woke up when Paul and Sally came home from school. They had heard about Josh's death from their teachers in their classes. He had been a friend to the whole family, so they, too, were sad.

"Will we still go to treatment?" Paul wondered out loud. A new wave of sadness touched Molly. What if this put a damper on the whole process? It would be hard enough getting help for Hank's alcoholism, much less dealing with the loss they all felt with Josh. Finally Paul's question filtered its way through her mind. She looked as if she just had a jolt.

"Oh! Yes, Paul. We can't wait with that," she said. "Josh would want us to continue, I know."

He would, she thought. She knew she couldn't postpone this now, or Hank might never get help.

When Bobbie and Ryan got home from school, she shared the news with them too. Bobbie went to her room and cried. Ryan simply sat and stared. Hank came home early as he had said he would, only to find the place like a morgue. He held Molly after she told him and she was surprised at his compassion.

"We don't have to go tonight, if you'd rather wait," he offered.

"No," she said firmly. "I think it's important that we start right now. It may even help us through this."

So they started treatment that night. They attended lectures and took part in a family therapy session. They also split off for individual and group meetings. The second night, they also visited the funeral parlor where Josh was being waked. Hank, however, stayed at the center. The counselor said he was beginning to have withdrawal symptoms from the alcohol. Hank swore it was the flu, but he agreed to stay anyway, which was a change in itself.

At the wake, Molly looked at Josh and spoke with several of her friends, colleagues and acquaintances, but it all seemed unreal to her.

The man she saw in the casket was not Josh. And, though she spoke about him to others, it seemed to her he would soon walk over and join the conversation as he always had at community functions.

CHAPTER XXI

THE funeral was Thursday. Hank left the treatment center, although he was still pretty sick, and even Scott came home from college. Molly sat at the organ and looked at her family all lined up in the pew. It was the first time Hank had been in church in years, and since the older kids had grown up they hadn't gone very often either. So this was perhaps the very first time they had all been there together in a long time.

She could tell even by the way they sat that something had changed. Scott sat on the end of the pew, a little apart from everyone else. Paul sat next to him and then Sally. Bobbie sat next to Sally and Ryan sat next to her. At the other end of the pew, close to Ryan, was Hank.

She wondered what would happen to each of them. Scott seemed distant from the family and even from his father. He looked depressed and his nose was running, though he didn't seem to have any other symptoms of a cold. Perhaps Molly was too suspicious, but she wondered about this cocaine epidemic that had supposedly hit the country and especially college campuses. It seemed particularly popular among intellectuals and athletes, and Scott fit into both categories.

She cringed at the thought of doing another intervention and she wondered if family ties would ever be that important to Scott.

Paul had seemed to make the biggest change so far. He had already brought a friend home after school. Sally seemed more confused than ever, but that was understandable with so many things happening so quickly. Bobbie had announced she had a date for Saturday night. Molly had consented, though she didn't like the boy. She wondered if Bobbie had traded taking care of Sally and Paul for taking care of Tom. But it was just a date and Molly tried not to make a big deal of it. Ryan seemed the same in some respects, but he did seem to be getting along much better with Hank.

As for Hank, he had expressed resentment at the way they had gotten him into treatment. But he did admit he couldn't think of what else might have done it. He had also told Molly in the privacy of their bedroom that he was going through treatment for his family's sake and still was not convinced he was an alcoholic, as the counselors seemed to be trying to tell him.

He said he thought he still might be able to drink socially. That idea really scared Molly, but she was learning, too, to take life one day at a time. He wasn't drinking now and he still had a month of treatment and A.A. meetings to go through. If he pretended long enough, and listened, maybe some things would rub off. She knew now that the family would handle it differently if he did drink again. She also thought she herself had changed, but she was a little vague as to how. It's always hardest to see yourself, she thought.

A cough startled her from her thoughts and she was surprised to see how the church had filled from the time her family had entered. She looked down at her watch and was startled to see that Fr. Brooks was waiting to start the service. She announced the entrance hymn and began to play.

Molly thought Fr. Brooks looked tired and sad as he proceeded through the service. She wondered if he had had the time to prepare a eulogy. She thought the worried look on his face indicated that he hadn't. At the eulogy, the priest paused for a moment and then began to speak in a rather apologetic voice.

"As I hope all of you can appreciate, I've been very busy over the last couple of days and haven't had much time to prepare words for this morning. I hope all of you know how much I loved this man and think that he deserves the very best. I won't use time as an excuse, however, because it was from a commitment to him that I didn't prepare anything. Instead I'll read a letter he had prepared and asked me to read." Fr. Brooks reached for a letter he had placed on the podium before the service.

"I've read this letter several times, hoping I could get through it without crying. I've yet to make it, so I doubt I'll do it this time." He cleared his throat, hoping it would cover up the fact that he had already started to cry.

My dear friends,
You probably thought you had heard the last of me, but here I am again speaking to you.

As I'm sure you have gathered by now, I wrote this before I died. You may think I'm going to tell you not to mourn, but I'm not. I spent too much of my life trying to talk people out of feelings, so I won't do it now. I loved you people and I think you loved me back, so it's only fitting that you grieve. It's good and healthy to grieve the loss of a loved one. I just don't want you grieving for the wrong reasons. So I'm trying to anticipate what you may be thinking as you cry.

Some of you may think I died too early, and there is a part of me that certainly agrees with that. Had I gone with the averages, I might have lived 15 more years. But I learned something too late in my life, and that is that sometimes it takes a crisis to make me move. Without the knowledge that I was dying, I would not have had the courage to ask you to sing, and you might not have been willing to sing. Now let me tell you this: I would not give up that Sunday when you sang my songs for anything—even 15 more years of the status quo.

I have been thinking about the words of that first song I asked you to sing, "Be not afraid; I go before you always. Come follow me."

I'd like you to follow me—not in dying, but in risking. I can't promise that all of your risks will pay off, but it beats living a life of fear or stagnation.

After that Sunday, I took some risks that didn't work, but I don't regret any of them. Sometimes I felt happy, sometimes sad, but always alive. You all risked singing the songs I wanted you to sing. Now I have one more request. Sing your own songs. Take the risk of living a creative life. Don't live a life praying for miracles. Go out and make one—or perhaps a dozen.

I am now on a new adventure that I'm excited about. As a Christian, I spent a lifetime preparing for this moment, so I don't want to run from it. I don't know if I'm allowed to keep an eye on you from where I'll be, but it would not fit my conception of heaven without that ability. I have spent the sixty plus years of my life involved in your lives. It is inconceivable to me that this would stop abruptly ... or ever, for that matter.

My conception of heaven would be that I'd be a mother eagle teaching you all to fly. Perhaps that's why I like that song "On Eagles' Wings" so much. I would fly each of you to the heavens, then drop you to earth. You would have to risk flying to save yourselves. With any luck you'd take off and fly on your own. But, if not, I'd swoop down and catch you on my back and take you safely back to the heavens. But soon I'd drop you again, till you could experience free flight. When you took your first solo I'd cry from the heavens and glory in your accomplishments. I also hope some day to be reunited with all of you.

But for now this is good-bye. And I love you.

FOREVER,

DR. JOSHUA KRUEGER

P.S. If you could find it in your heart to sing "Be Not Afraid" one more time I'll do my best to listen wherever I may be.

P.P.S. I wouldn't mind "On Eagles' Wings" at the end, either.

About halfway through the letter, the priest gave up trying to stop crying and let the tears flow. After the sermon he said, "I really don't know what I can add to that. Certainly that letter speaks to the man that he was. You can bet at the proper moment I'll be singing 'Be Not Afraid.' I hope you'll join me."

When the time came, Molly announced the song and the people tried singing. It was not as loud as that first Sunday with Josh, even though the church was more full. It wasn't that the people didn't try. They did. It was just hard to sing through the tears. People's mouths would open but a sob rather than a song would emerge.

They sang "On Eagles' Wings" on the way out of church. Perhaps walking helped, but for whatever reason, they sang louder.

CHAPTER **XXII**

THE family had finished treatment and school was out for the summer before Molly was ready to visit Josh's grave. She went at a time, in the heat of the day, when she was sure of being alone. She had the windows down in the car. This summer, for some reason, she didn't use her air conditioning. Nothing felt better to her than allowing the sights, sounds, and smells of summer to wash over her. A car passed her with a dog sticking his head out the window, and she wished she could do the same. She wished, too, that she could walk and talk with her friend rather than standing over his grave. She missed talking to him and telling him about the family and what each one was doing.

So when she stopped to visit his grave she chatted with him much the way she would have if he'd been alive.

"I'm so sorry, old friend. It's been so long without my visiting you. I guess it's hard for me to do two things at once. I've been so busy with my family since the intervention, I just haven't had time. Nor, I guess, did I have the courage to face my feelings for you.

"You sure were right about so many things. First about risk. It was scary to do that intervention! And there has been pain and sadness as well as joy as a result of it. But it certainly did produce change. Scott still seems distant from the family and I'm more convinced than ever he has problems with drugs. But Hank and I have been talking openly about it. Hank is less convinced than I am, but he did say the other night we should confront Scott with our concerns.

"Bobbie is still dating Tom. He's less of a jerk than I thought, but I still hope she doesn't settle on anyone for a long time. I wish she could just have fun for a while, and not be so darned serious. Ryan is still angry and fights a lot, but both he and Bobbie are attending Al-Ateen and also a new group called Adult Children of Alcoholics that seems to be helping them. It is the older children that seem more 'stuck' in their patterns.

"Paul and Sally seem more flexible and more trusting of the changes. Paul has two boys now that he pals around with. He seems to like it best when they call him, but he enjoys their company enough that, if he doesn't see them for awhile, he calls them. Sally is still a clown, but she seems willing to live with tension a little more rather than making a joke to relieve it. She also seems to have her feet on the ground more and is not running in a million different directions like she use to be.

"As for me, you were right there, too. Hank wants more of my time now. Sometimes I enjoy it, but others I'd rather be with my music. He also wants to be more involved with the children and I feel a little jealous about the place that he's taking in their hearts and lives. Yet my worst fear is that he'll drink again. Each night, even if he's five minutes late, I picture him in the bar. I realize more and more that I was as involved in alcohol as he was, and in many ways I think it'll take me longer to recover. I'm still afraid of my feelings. I still go to Al-Anon meetings, but it still seems as though the others' lives are so different from mine. I know that's denial, but it seems so hard to break through.

"But enough about my family, dear friend. It's time that you and I talk. You and I talk! Listen to me. You can't talk. I don't even know if you can listen. But you taught me to hope again, and I can hope that you can hear this. I also hope you can understand it, because I don't know if I do.

"The worst part of where I was is that I didn't know my own feelings. I'm angry at you for not trusting more in our friendship and not being more willing to risk that sooner than you did. Believe it or not, I'm not sad for me that it didn't happen sooner. I'm not even sure it would have worked sooner. But I am sad for you, because I wish you could have been a part of it. As the family doctor you could have added a lot, and I sure could have used your support.

"I just wish you could have at least the pleasure of hearing me say 'thank you' for teaching me to risk again, and for pushing me to do the intervention. Because, in spite of the pain, I think the whole family and I are healthier for it. Even if Hank should go back to drinking, I know we would cope with it differently.

"But the anger was just the first feeling. It didn't take me long to forgive you, dear friend. After all, even doctors have a right to be human.

Besides, when I thought about it more, I felt guilty. I realized you may not have trusted in our friendship because I never let you know how I felt about you. Even worse, I never let myself know how I felt. I'm beginning to realize that I may have grown up in an alcoholic family myself. I didn't want my children to grow up in a family without talk, trust, or feeling the way I now realize that my brothers and sister and I did, but that's exactly what was happening before you pushed me to do something about it. I couldn't let you know about my feelings because I couldn't face them myself.

"So, dear friend, don't feel guilty for eternity that you didn't confront me soon enough. I should be thanking you for letting me experience closeness in a friendship, even if I did realize too late how important it was to me. Maybe I can have that closeness with others now, thanks to you. But I'll wish forever that I could have told you before you died and that I would have had at least a short time to experience it with you."

For the first time since Josh's death, Molly really let all her feelings go. She knelt down by his grave and pounded the ground. "Why did you have to die without knowing how I felt about you?" she sobbed.

Suddenly she heard a cry in the sky. She looked high above her and an eagle soared. The bird cried again. Molly never saw coincidence in the same way again.